Brain-Based Learning With Class

COLLEEN POLITANO
JOY PAQUIN

WITH A FOREWORD BY ERIC JENSEN

PORTAGE & MAIN PRESS
(PEGUIS PUBLISHERS)

Winnipeg • Canada

Portage & Main Press acknowledges the financial support of the Government of Canada through the Book Publishing Industry Development Program (BPIDP) for our publishing activities.

Printed and bound in Canada by Kromar Printing

00 01 02 03 04 5 4 3 2 1

Canadian Cataloguing in Publication Data
Politano, Colleen, 1946-

    Brain-based learning with class

    Includes bibliographical references.
    ISBN 1-894110-48-X

1. Learning, Psychology of. 2. Teaching—Psychological aspects. 3. Brain—Study and teaching. I. Paquin, Joy, 1947- II. Title.

LB1060.P64 1999   370.15'23   C99-920218-9

Book and cover design: Suzanne Gallant
Cover and text illustrations: Jess Dixon
Photographs: Colleen and Leon Politano, Joy and Paul Paquin

PORTAGE & MAIN PRESS
(Peguis Publishers)

100-318 McDermot Avenue
Winnipeg, Manitoba, Canada R3A 0A2
Email: books@peguis.com
Tel.: 204-987-3500
Toll free: 800-667-9673
Fax: 204-947-0080

We have learned that brains work best when there is emotional support, appropriate challenge, and instant feedback. Our families—Leon Politano; Mary Pat and Sally Johnston; Paul, Rebecca, John, and Ben Paquin; and Bernice Johnston—have given us all these and more. With love, we dedicate our book to them.

—Colleen and Joy

Contents

Acknowledgments

Learning about the brain is a multi-faceted process. We thank our students and our colleagues who allow us to learn with and from them. We thank the authors whose works have informed and inspired us, in particular, Geoffrey and Renata Caine, Marilyn Chapman, Marian Diamond, Carla Hannaford, Eric Jensen, Susan Kovalik, Candace Pert, V.S. Ramachandran, Richard Restak and Daniel Schacter, David Sousa, and Robert Sylwester. We thank the workshop presenters Barrie Bennett, Don Campbell, Eric Jensen, Susan Kovalik, V.S. Ramachandran, David Sousa, Robert Sylwester, and Pat Wolfe for showing us the power and the possibilities of using information about the brain to inform our classroom practice. Finally, our utmost thanks to Eric Jensen who opened the doors for us through his writings, summer seminars, and mentorship.

Writing a book is also a process that needs the support of many people. We would like to thank our friends for their understanding and encouragement while we were writing. Our thanks go to Caren Cameron, Paul Paquin, Anne Davies, Marilyn Chapman, George Urban, Jody Bain, and Eric Jensen for responding to our manuscript; and to our teaching colleagues Fran Beckow and Jennifer Davidson for being so willing to implement brain-based learning with us. As well, thanks to Leigh Hambly, our editor, for her expertise and patience.

Foreword

Every teacher wants to do a better job, but the job description seems to be ever expanding. Teachers have become surrogate parents, counselors, technologists, team players, learners, and presenters. Now you can add to that list one who must keep up with the latest in brain research. Recent discoveries are helping us understand how kids learn and why they don't learn. These discoveries can help us understand the mechanisms and possibilities of meaning-making and memory. And so, for the first time in history, we can begin to make classroom adjustments based on this research.

But a fundamental problem remains. Who has the time to find, decipher, and make practical all the latest discoveries in brain research? The answer is that most teachers simply don't have the time. Fortunately to you, the reader, Joy Paquin and Colleen Politano have made the time in their busy schedules to learn about the brain. More important, after they began that journey, they have diligently implemented their discoveries and documented what works and what doesn't.

The book you have in your hands, *Brain-Based Learning With Class*, is the result of a tremendous amount of work, insights, and thoughtful consideration. While the book does have some measured, purposeful information about the three-pound miracle resting on our shoulders, what the book really does best is give you practical, specific applications of that research in easy, ready-to-use, teacher-friendly formats.

This book was a joy to read. I'm certain you'll find the book both enjoyable and, most of all, a real boost to learning, student enjoyment, and improved performance. Bon appetit!

Eric Jensen

Introduction

Why This Book?

Teachers are busy people. We know. We each have a family, work full time in our own classroom, facilitate workshops, and write books and articles. Like all teachers, we want to do our best for our students and we want our students to be successful. We have found that success through brain-based learning. We discovered that the more we learned about the brain and the more we applied that knowledge to our practice, the more positive results we began to see. Our experiences in implementing brain-based learning in the classroom have enabled us to share ideas that are easily accomplished and produce great results.

For the past few years, we have been presenting workshops about applying brain-based ideas in the classroom. Workshop participants tell us our ideas are effective, useful, teacher-friendly, and "kid-busy." Many participants asked us to put our ideas into a book. At first, we wondered, what can we offer that has not already been written about? Educators told us—they wanted a book that provides basic background information about the brain, ways to teach students about the brain, and practical brain-based activities.

When we decided to write this book, we had two goals in mind. One was to help educators teach their students about the brain and how learning works; the second was to show ways in which brain-based learning can have a positive effect on all aspects of classroom life. We believe we have succeeded.

What Is Brain-Based Learning?

Brain-based learning is a natural, motivating, and positive way of maximizing learning and teaching. It is an approach that is based on the ways our brain learns best.

Over the past thirty years, new technology has resulted in a dramatic increase in the information available about the brain. A growing number of educators are looking at the current work of neuroscientists and trying to use that information to support and inform classroom practice. Although brain research may not "prove" anything, it gives us a way to think about what we already do, what we need to do more of, and what we need to reconsider. Articles about the brain are appearing in popular magazines on a regular basis, leading parents of students to ask us questions about the connection between what they are reading about the brain and what we do. As educators, we need to be informed, thoughtful, articulate, and active in using relevant information to enhance learning in our classrooms.

The Framework for a Brain-Based Environment

There is an almost overwhelming amount of information available about the brain. The problem is—where to start? We looked at the work of educators such as Renate Caine and Geoffrey Caine, Robert Sylwester, Pat Wolfe, Susan Kovalik, and Eric Jensen. All suggest ways to apply information about the brain to support and enhance learning. The work of these educators provided us with valuable information.

In his summer seminar, "An Introduction of Brain-Based Learning and Teaching," Eric Jensen presented ten important principles that need to be implemented for a brain-compatible approach to teaching and learning. We adapted these principles to be our brain basics because they gave us a comprehensive framework for our approach to the practical application of brain-based learning.

The factors we consider to be basic to creating a brain-based environment are: uniqueness, assessment, emotions, meaning, multi-path, brain-body, memory, nutrition, cycles and rhythms, and elimination of threat. We use these factors for thinking about brain-based learning, planning instruction, and designing activities for our students.

What's In It for Me?

One of the first questions we learned to ask on our brain-based journey was, WIIFM (pronounced wif-um)—What's in it for me? In *Quantum Learning*, Bobbi DePorter and Mike Hernacki stress the importance of helping students see the relevance of learning activities. So, we began by asking ourselves, "WIIFM?" Colleen wanted to gather scientific information about the brain to support her classroom practice with the credibility and authority that comes from a medical-scientific model, but in a language everyone could understand. Joy wanted to know why things that consistently worked so well in classrooms, worked as well as they did. We each started with a specific goal in mind but quickly discovered there were much greater implications. The more we learned, the more we realized how much more there was, and still is, to learn. Applying what we have learned so far has improved the quality of life and learning in our classrooms. We hope this is your experience.

Now, whenever we begin something new, we ask ourselves the WIIFM question. Whenever we start a new topic or theme with our students, we begin by having them think about WIIFM. By identifying some reasons for doing an activity or unit of study, we become more focused and committed. When students feel that an activity is purposeful and worth their time and effort, they are more likely to become motivated and actively involved. Sometimes relevance is easy to see; other times it just takes some searching and imagination.

Tackling a complex topic like the brain takes persistence and dedication. We have found that having someone to talk to—to share ideas and build enthusiasm with—has kept us going and improved our learning. We encourage you to find a partner or group of interested educators so that you can work through the activities, share ideas, and celebrate successes together.

Activity: What's In It For Me? (WIIFM)

Why

To establish personal relevance and purpose

How

- Think about why learning about the brain might be worth your time.

- Learn about the brain.

- If you are doing this with a partner, share your ideas.

- Record your personal WIIFM.

- Take time to go back and check your WIIFM notes.

Show What You Already Know

We learn best when we make personal connections to what we already know. Every learner is unique and has prior knowledge. We need to recognize our experience base and build on it. The best way to make learning meaningful is by starting with what we already know. We can use meaning and memory maps, posters, drawings, diagrams, lists, or other ways of representing. These representations become the baseline or launching pad for exploring concepts.

Activity: Show What You Already Know (SWYAK)

Why

To establish prior knowledge

How

- Record (web, list, mind-map, diagram) what you already know about the brain.

- If you have a partner to work with, share your representation.

- Add to your representation as you learn new information.

How to Use This Book

The brain basics have also provided us with a structure for organizing this book. In Part 1, we introduce the ten brain basics and give a summary of information about the brain. In Part 2, we give educators suggestions for teaching a theme or unit on the brain, including how to introduce students to the brain basics. In Part 3, the brain basics are the framework for practical activities educators can use to create and enhance brain-friendly classrooms. In Part 4, we include suggestions for using the brain basics as a guide for assessing and planning in brain-compatible classrooms.

> *Students of all ages can do the activities throughout the book.*
> *Decide on the level of detail appropriate for your classes.*

We are sure the ideas on the pages that follow will work for you. Build on them, add to them, and shape them to fit your needs. In workshops, we urge participants to "adapt, not adopt." Please do the same with the ideas in this book.

Learning About the Brain

Learning about the brain gives us the foundation we need to teach our students about their learning. As teachers, we need to give our students accurate information and use correct terminology that will become common language in the classroom. As we learn more about the brain, we are more able to appreciate its complexity and power.

In chapter 1, Describing the Brain, we present a brief description of the brain. The information presented in chapter 2, Learning in Action, helps us understand how learning happens. With this understanding, we can develop a more purposeful orientation to our own learning, and we can design more appropriate learning environments for our students. In chapter 3, Introducing the Brain Basics, we provide background information for each of the ten areas we consider "basic" when creating brain-compatible learning environments. This information will help educators think about their knowledge and apply that knowledge to their practice.

CHAPTER ONE

Describing the Brain

Parts of the Brain

The brain is complicated; learning about how the brain works is complicated. Everything in our brain is interconnected and interrelated to everything else in our body. For the purpose of learning, though, we need to separate the brain into manageable chunks or categories. Although we attribute certain functions to different areas of the brain, we know the brain works as a whole.

When we look at a model of the brain, we can view it from outside and inside and from different angles. We can look at its two sides, four lobes, and outer brain, midbrain, and lower brain regions.

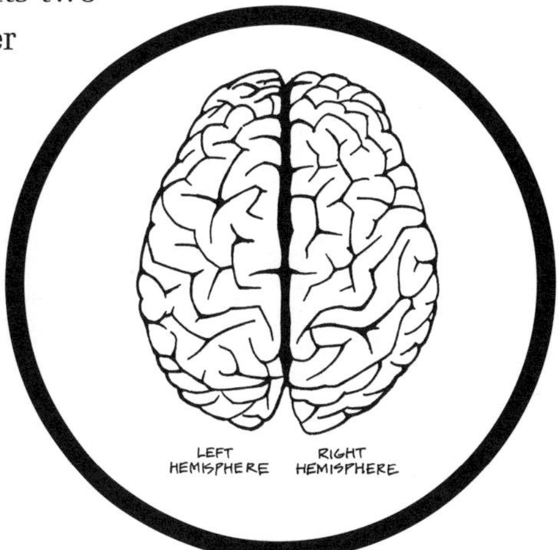

The Hemispheres

left hemisphere: thought to process logical sequencing, reasoned judgments, literal interpretations, and language-related ideas; gives structure and order to thoughts, classifies ideas, deals with numbers and calculations, and provides critical analysis of ideas; controls the right side of the body

Figure 1.
The hemispheres
(Reproducible master in appendix)

right hemisphere: thought to process visual patterns and images (graphs, maps, and cartoons), spatial information, and spontaneous, random, and open-ended ideas; uses intuition, deals with novelty, paradox, and ambiguity; controls the left side of the body

The Four Lobes

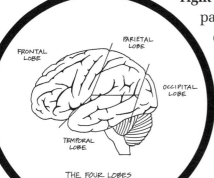

Figure 2.
The four lobes
(Reproducible master in appendix)

frontal lobe: located in the front of the brain; the center for planning, creativity, problem solving, and judgment; integration of cognition, emotion, and senses

temporal lobe: located on both the left side and right side of the brain above and around the ears; responsible for language, making meaning, memory, and hearing

parietal lobe: located at the top of the brain toward the back; deals with sensory and language functions

occipital lobe: located at the back of the brain above the cerebellum; concerned with vision

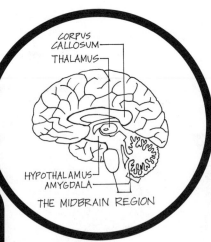

The Brain From the Outside In

skull: the hollow wall of bone that protects the brain

cerebrospinal fluid: clear fluid that surrounds the brain and spinal cord and protects the brain from damage; carries nutrients to the brain and removes waste products

meninges (dura mater, arachnoid, pia mater): three thin coverings that wrap around the brain, cushioning and protecting it

cerebral cortex: the wrinkled outer layer of the cerebrum made of six layers of neurons packed tightly together; cortex comes from the Latin for "bark" (of a tree)

Figure 3.
The brain from the outside in
(Reproducible master in appendix)

The Midbrain Region

corpus callosum: early assumptions about left and right brain lateralization are outdated. The corpus callosum, a dense band of more than 250 million axons, connects the two hemispheres and allows each side of the brain to exchange information freely with the other side.

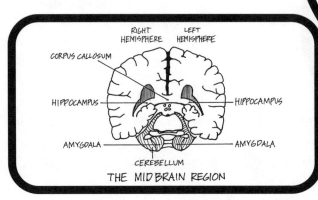

Figure 4.
The midbrain region
(Reproducible master in appendix)

Brain-Based Learning With Class

thalamus: receives information from the senses and relays it to other parts of the brain

hypothalamus: the brain's thermostat; controls appetite, digestion, circulation, sleep, hormone secretion, sexuality, and emotions

hippocampus: plays a major role in consolidating learning by transferring information from working memory to long-term retention. This structure is critical to meaning.

amygdala: an almond-shaped structure connected to the hippocampus; responsible for processing sensory information and for coding the brain's emotional memories

The Lower Brain

brain stem: located at the top of the spinal cord; links lower brain and midbrain, controls heartbeat, digestion, and body temperature

medulla oblongata: channels information between the spinal cord and the brain; controls respiration, circulation, wakefulness, and heart rate

pons: located at the top of the brain stem; relay station for sensory information

reticular formation: a netlike formation of nuclei running up the brain stem from the medulla oblongata through the pons and midbrain; controls levels of alertness, respiration, cardiovascular function, digestion, and sleep patterns; regulates information from the senses to the neocortex

cerebellum: sometimes known as the "little brain," the cerebellum is located behind the brain stem; involved in movement, posture, coordination, balance, motor memory (for example, a golf swing, catching a ball, shaking someone's hand), and novelty learning

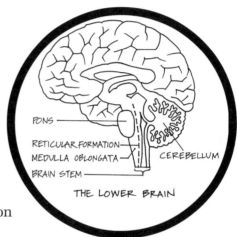

Figure 5.
The lower brain
(Reproducible master in appendix)

CHAPTER TWO

Learning in Action

How Cells Communicate

One of the fascinating things about the brain is the way the cells communicate. When we think about how learning happens, we think of what happens between cells, on the receptor sites, and through peptides.

Our brain contains glial cells and neurons. The glial cells, or worker cells, have no cell body and outnumber neurons ten to one. They carry nutrients, remove dead cells, give structural support, and help to regulate the immune system. Neurons communicate in a cell-to-cell process. Each neuron is made up of a cell body with multiple branches called dendrites and one long extension called an axon. Neurons are separated from one another by a gap called a synapse.

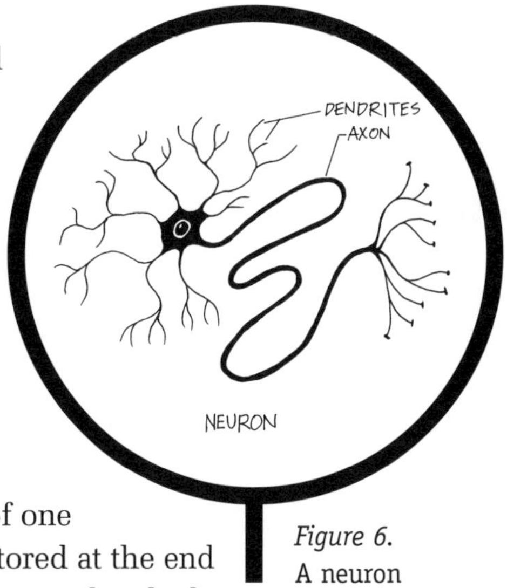

DENDRITES
AXON

NEURON

Figure 6.
A neuron
(Reproducible master in appendix)

When an electrical impulse travels along the axon of one neuron, it triggers the release of neurotransmitters stored at the end of the axon. These neurotransmitters are absorbed by receptor sites at the ends of dendrites that are connected to another neuron and the link is made between the cells. One cell may connect with as many as 50 000 other cells. The neuron stays put while the axon can extend to up to a meter (three feet) in length. The thicker the axon is, the faster it conducts information. Well-used axons are myelinated. Myelin is a fatty substance that forms around the axon, speeding up electrical transmission and reducing interference from other nearby reactions.

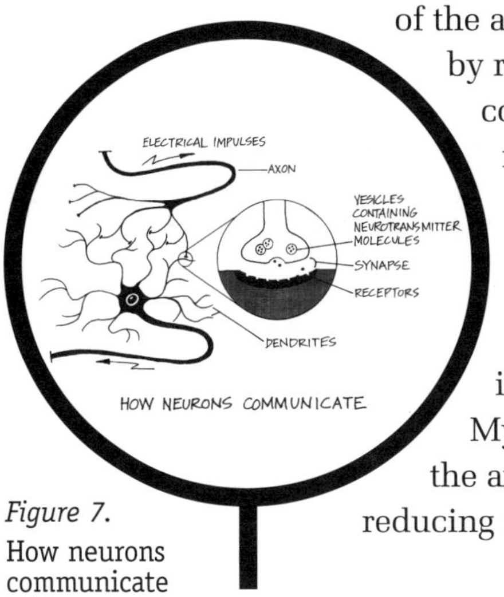

ELECTRICAL IMPULSES

AXON

VESICLES CONTAINING NEUROTRANSMITTER MOLECULES

SYNAPSE

RECEPTORS

DENDRITES

HOW NEURONS COMMUNICATE

Figure 7.
How neurons communicate
(Reproducible master in appendix)

> *When we teach our students about myelination, they become very aware of "making connections."*

In the past, much of what was written and talked about regarding the way learning happens focused on the cell-to-cell stimulation that occurs in the brain. Recent work in neuroscience, however, has established that this process accounts for less than 2 percent of the body's total communication.

In addition to the receptor sites that are located at the end of each dendrite, receptor sites are also located on neurons. Each neuron has several million of these surface opiate-receptors, each of which is a single molecule made up of proteins. The receptors function as sensing molecules waiting to bind with the right chemicals, called ligands. This binding is a lock-and-key arrangement. The agitator or ligand is the chemical key and the receptor site is the lock. Although the ligands may be common synaptic neurotransmitters, 95 percent of the time they are peptides.

Coming to Terms With the Brain's Connections

glia: the worker cells (interneurons). The glia, which outnumber neurons ten to one, have no cell body. They carry nutrients, help regulate the immune systems, remove dead cells, and give structural support.

neuron: one of two types of brain cells; made up of a cell body, an axon, and dendrites

dendrites: the many branch-like extensions from the neuron cell body. The ends of the dendrites are the receptor sites for axons.

axon: the one long fiber per neuron that extends from the neuron. The axon carries electrical nerve impulses to the dendrites of other neurons. Although there is just one axon per neuron, the axon can subdivide with many dendrites.

synapse: the gap where chemicals are released to stimulate or inhibit the communication between axons and dendrites

myelin: a white, fatty substance that coats the axons. This insulation speeds up the transmission of messages between cells.

neurotransmitters: biochemical messengers that are released at the synapse. Neurotransmitters excite neurons to receive messages, or they inhibit the process. Neurotransmitters are grouped into three categories: (1) amino acids such as glutamate and gaba (principle neurotransmitters that carry excitatory or inhibitory signals), (2) monoamines such as dopamine, serotonin, and norepinephrine (determine whether the signal will be excitatory or inhibitory), and (3) peptides such as endorphin and vasopressin (affect behavior patterns).

electrical impulses: the messages that travel in one direction from the cell body down the axon to the synapse, stimulating the release of neurotransmitters

protein: a compound made up of one or more chains of amino acids. Proteins, a fundamental part of all living cells, include many substances such as enzymes, hormones, and antibodies.

amino acids: the chief component of proteins and smaller peptides. Derived from ammonia, they join together in long chains to form proteins.

ligands: informational substances including neurotransmitters, hormones, steroids, and peptides, which bind with receptors in a lock-and-key arrangement

peptides: chains of amino acids that travel throughout the body acting as the messengers of our emotional system

receptor sites: protein molecules situated in the outer membrane that bind with ligands to make brain-body communication possible

Brain-Based Learning With Class

Peptides are distributed throughout the body and the brain as strings of amino acid receptors on neurons. These informational substances travel throughout our body and brain in our neural networks, circulatory system, and bloodstream. They act as the primary source of information transfer for as much as 98 percent of all communications. Peptides are now being referred to as the body's second nervous system and the molecules of emotion. Candace Pert (1997) compares the cell-to-cell communication process to cellular phones and suggests the peptide process is more like the noise from huge bullhorns with a total body broadcast range. She says, "Our entire body thinks, not just our brain."

Introducing the Brain Basics

Uniqueness

The emerging message is clear: The brain, with its complex architecture and limitless potential, is a highly plastic, constantly changing entity that is powerfully shaped by our experiences in childhood and throughout life.

— Marian Diamond and Janet Hopson, *Magic Trees of the Mind*

Our brains, like our fingerprints, are unique. Even identical twins who come from the same environment have very different brains. We are the products of both our genetics and our environment. There is no longer a controversy about "nature" versus "nurture"; each contributes to who we are. Not only is our nervous system customized, so is our emotional system. When students walk through our classroom doors we need to consider who each is and where each has been.

We know our students have different learning styles, learning senses, and learning strengths. With this understanding, we must have wide expectations both for who our students are and for what they are able to do.

There are critical periods of neural plasticity, or "windows of opportunity," in which the brain is more physiologically wired to learn. The period from birth to three years is critical for establishing vision, language, muscle control, and emotional and intellectual development. The experiences, or lack of experiences, children have in their early years when the plasticity of the brain is most malleable impact their learning. Children (between birth and three years) who miss the window of opportunity because they did not receive stimulation can still learn, but they find it more difficult.

Our goal is to get to know our students so we can help them build on what they already know; for those whose experiences have been limited, we try to provide the rich experiences necessary for them to construct their understandings. We realize that comparisons between students are pointless because of the huge range of abilities and experiences each has. We have learned that a three-year range in development is normal.

How can we help each student be successful when we are confronted with the reality of his or her uniqueness? During our teaching careers, we have moved from the "one lesson fits all" technique to the other extreme—trying to create an individual program for each student in our classrooms. We discovered that each extreme involved "craziness."

The first method drove our students crazy because our expectation was that everyone could do the same thing at the same time in the same way. It also drove us crazy because the lessons turned out to be too difficult for one-third of the students, too easy for one-third of the students, and okay for the last one-third. We did not want to set up two-thirds of our students to have behavior or learning problems. Our friend Caren Cameron refers to this type of organization as a "TIC" (teacher-initiated crisis).

The second method drove us crazy because we could not possibly keep up with designing and monitoring a program for each student. The lack of structure and community was often unsettling for students. Sylvia Kane, a wonderful teacher who at one stage in her career tried to run individualized programs in her classroom, likens this style of teaching to students picking fruit from the "tree of knowledge" when they were ready. Some students had the tree picked bare in two days while others refused to even walk by the tree.

We have learned that when we design activities that have students actively engaged in constructing and representing their understanding, they are not only busy, they are learning. We describe this as "shared experience, individual response." We plan our lessons so that we begin with a whole-group activity, then we give the students several choices of ways to process their thinking and then represent their learning. This allows each student to work on the same concept while permitting each to work in ways that most suit his or her learning style and developmental stage. When we give students choice in showing what they know, our classrooms are "teacher friendly, kid busy!"

> *We are committed to working in multi-aged classrooms because the mixture of ages takes the focus off the need for sameness, and supports the uniqueness of individual learners.*

When we reflected on what worked well for our students, we realized there was a pattern. Successful lessons and activities have two elements—*choice and variety.* Throughout this book, choice and variety becomes an often repeated phrase. We realize we can accommodate the wide range of needs, learning styles, learning senses, and abilities in our students by providing choice and variety. Younger students need more variety and fewer choices; older students need less variety and more choices. When planning, we design lessons with enough scope to appeal to the uniqueness of learners in our classrooms and provide choices that allow students to think and learn in the ways that are best for them. The question we ask ourselves is not, How can we teach it best? but, How can our students learn best?

Assessment

People will overachieve targets they set for themselves.

— Gordon Dryden, *Out of the Red*

Assessment is crucial to learning. Assessment done well provides feedback that the brain needs. Done poorly, assessment may inhibit the brain's ability to function well. We cannot possibly know what our students think or can do until they represent their learning. When we observe the processes students use as they are working, when we look at the products they create, and when we talk with them about their thinking and their feelings, we learn about our students. With this approach of broad-based assessment, we learn not only about their products, but we also learn about the way they work and their attitudes toward tasks. We know that students with positive attitudes are more likely to learn. This process of observing, collecting, and conversing over time gives us the evidence we need to evaluate and support students and to plan what we will do next.

> *Assessment is gathering evidence; evaluation is making professional judgments based on the evidence.*

Some forms of assessment are more brain-friendly than others. We strive to make assessment authentic because it provides useful information about and for our learners. Done in the context of classroom learning, authentic assessment provides an accurate description of what students have learned. We know that a three-year range in development is normal. If we know our students and their stages of development, we can appreciate their efforts, understand where they have come from, and help them move forward. Authentic evidence is embedded in the learning activities that happen in the classroom. The closer the assessment activity is to the everyday routines students are familiar with, the more authentic and dynamic it is. The more separated the assessment activity is from everyday routines, the less authentic it is. Marilyn Chapman (1997), in *Weaving Webs of Meaning*, describes a continuum of authenticity. She rates ongoing observations, conversations, conferences, and performance assessments as most authentic and rates formal written tests, timed tests, multiple-choice tests, and group-administered standardized achievement tests as the least authentic. Activities that are done within the normal routines of the classroom are less threatening, while unfamiliar activities and formats can be threatening to many students. There will be times when our students are involved in less authentic assessment activities. As teachers, we can help alleviate the stress and anxiety by giving them practice opportunities, and by teaching them relaxation techniques and "test-wise" strategies.

The more ways and choices students have to show what they know, the greater chance we have of gaining accurate information about what they have learned. As well as representation being a key to assessment, we know that as students represent their learning, they create meaning and understanding. Bruner (1996, 23) states, "The process of thought and its product become interwoven." We encourage our students to develop a repertoire of representing that includes: talking, movement, drama, dance, songs, gestures, projects, drawings, paintings, collages, mind maps, graphs, charts, models, and different forms of writing.

Assessment informs evaluation, which drives instruction and the choices we make about when and what we focus on in the prescribed curriculum. Assessment provides specific information that enables us to support each learner by discovering who needs help, who needs further challenge, who needs extra practice, and who is ready to move on. Assessment and evaluation are vital parts of the teaching-learning cycle. We share information with students and parents through reporting, and then set goals that drive our teaching. The process of assessing, evaluating, teaching, and learning is an ongoing cycle.

Establishing criteria with students before an assignment or some activities reduces anxiety and helps more students be successful. This does not have to be an arduous process. When we take a few moments to talk about what quality looks like and to list the main points, students have a clearer vision of what they are aiming toward. When students know the criteria, they have a feeling of control.

Our own memories of assessment in school are not pleasant. We recall some assessment as punitive and manipulative. We felt we were sometimes tricked and the goal seemed to be to establish what we did *not* know, rather than to find out what we did know. Often, assessment and evaluation were used to rank students. Our goal is to use assessment and evaluation as tools to help students learn better.

When we start talking about assessment and evaluation in workshops, some participants begin to squirm. It all seems overwhelming! If we evaluate on our own, it ends up being what Jensen (1996) describes as, "too little, too late and too vague!" We say, share the responsibilities, let some of it go to where it really belongs—to the students themselves! When we include students in the assessment-evaluation process, we reduce our workload and we teach our students to be reflective and responsive. Students learn to think about their own efforts and learn to be constructive in responding to the work of their peers. As we include students in self-assessment and peer-assessment, they learn to be specific and to provide information that makes a difference.

> **As adults, we sometimes have difficulty accepting compliments and criticisms. With positive assessment practices, students learn early on to listen to and accept compliments and criticisms, not react to them.**

Emotions

> *...emotions are the gatekeepers to the intellect....*
> *emotional hooks are necessary for long-term learning;*
> *negative emotions can become blocks to learning.*
>
> — Robin Fogarty, *Brain-Compatible Classrooms*

Traditionally, emotion and learning have been viewed as two separate entities in most school cultures. Educators whose classrooms worked well followed their intuition by taking care of the emotional aspects of the learning environment. Current brain research shows that this instinctive wisdom was right. If we do not pay attention to emotions, we miss a powerful opportunity to make learning meaningful and relevant and may, in fact, unwittingly block learning.

We now have a scientific basis to justify making emotions a factor in planning learning experiences. Three themes have emerged from the research: (1) emotions have their own pathways or superhighways in our body, (2) emotions affect brain chemicals, and (3) emotions influence learning and memory.

It was once thought that the whole midbrain, or limbic brain, which is part of the limbic system, was the center of emotions. However, current research has found that the amygdala is the structure of the brain most involved in emotions. Joseph LeDoux (1996), recognized as an expert on the "emotional brain," explains that the amygdala matures before the cortex. Emotions from our earliest, intense, experiences—particularly fear—may affect us long-term if these experiences happened when our brain was immature and we had not developed the thinking capacity to understand the implications of the situation.

The most talked about form of communication within our brain is the electrical-chemical-electrical process between neurons. Emotions trigger the chemicals active in the axon-synapse-dendrite reaction, inhibiting or allowing communication between cells. Chemicals also act on the surface of the neurons. Neurons are covered with millions of opiate receptors that function as sensing molecules. They bind with agitator chemicals called ligands in a lock-and-key arrangement. According to Candace Pert (1997), Miles Herkenham at NIH says, "The majority of communication (98 percent) is carried out by peptides." Peptides are strings of amino acids that travel throughout the blood stream and act as a primary source of information transfer. Sylwester (1995) calls peptides, "the messengers of our emotional system" and suggests we think of our emotions as "the glue that integrates our body and brain, and peptide molecules as the physical manifestation of the process." Pert's research on peptides helps us understand intuition or "gut feelings." The chemicals of emotion influence most of our behaviors and remain in our body after an emotional experience. This helps us to understand why it is hard for us to let go of our feelings long after an incident has passed.

Learning is strongly affected by emotion. Our emotions drive attention, health, learning, and memory. The stronger the emotion connected with an experience, the stronger the memory of that experience. Emotion helps us to focus, set priorities and goals, and make value-based decisions.

As educators, we know we cannot ignore emotions. Learning and memory are hindered and discipline problems may occur when emotions are suppressed. It is just as counterproductive to randomly trigger extreme emotion in our students. Instead, we need to plan appropriate activities that use emotion to our learners' advantage.

We try to be aware of the emotional states of our students and to help them develop self-control and strategies for dealing with their emotions. The clues to the way our students are feeling are evident in the state they are in or in the way they present themselves. When our students are in positive states of emotion, they are more likely to learn and remember.

When our students are in negative states, we need to help them move into a state more conducive to learning. In his seminars, Jensen says, "Good teachers are good managers of their students' states." Ways to help students get into a positive emotional state are to have them talk, move, and reflect. Modeling love of learning and creating a classroom environment where rituals and celebration are dealt with are foundations for emotional well-being.

Meaning

A mind stretched to a new idea never returns
from its original dimensions.

— Oliver Wendell Holmes, in *The Teacher's Quotation Book*

To the brain, making meaning is more important than receiving information. When we are bombarded with information the brain is less able to sort important information. Rather than responding to an avalanche of data, the brain copes by dealing with only what is meaningful. The brain makes meaning through patterns, relevance, and emotions. Without meaning, we are dealing with bits of isolated data; when we can make meaning, we can assemble the data and make sense of it.

Our brain is a superb patternmaker. Through the senses, the brain constantly scans the environment looking for patterns and connections so that new information links with current knowledge and understandings. As each pattern is established, it is added to the brain's "perceptual maps" for future reference. Patterning allows us to organize and associate new information with what we already know. Context is vital for meaning-making because without the whole picture assorted bits of information do not make sense. We learn best when we have the big picture, real-life connections, and conceptual, thematic learning. Our brain creates relevance by making connections between experiences and existing neural sites. The more relevant the material is to the learner, the greater meaning the material has. Emotion is critical to meaning. Emotions are triggered by the brain's chemistry and they signal to the brain "this is important." When we ignore emotion, we risk meaning.

There are two kinds of meaning: surface and deeply felt (Caine, Caine, and Crowell 1994). Surface meaning is more literal; some people refer to literal questions as "skinny" questions (Fogarty 1997, 88). We refer to these questions as "no brainers." Joy's favorite example is, What color is the red truck? Deep meaning involves more critical/creative thinking. If we want our students to consider big-picture issues, we need to ask and encourage students to ask "fat" questions.

Learners need time to make meaning. One of the phrases we use over and over comes from Eric Jensen, "You can have your learners' attention, or they can be making meaning, but not at the same time." If students are going to move from surface meaning to deep internalized meaning, they need opportunities to talk, reflect, and apply what they are learning. As teachers, we must remember each of our students is unique. The connections a student makes may be very different from the connections other students make and the connections that we make. What is meaningful depends on who we are and the experiences we have had. This really brings home the phrase, "there are no wrong answers."

Multi-Path

> Hand-in-glove with an accurately evolving description of each person's intelligence is the need for an educational regime that helps every person to achieve his or her maximum potential across the range of disciplines and crafts.
>
> — Howard Gardner, *Multiple Intelligences*

The more ways we present information, the more chances we give our students to understand and remember material. In an attempt to be efficient, educators often organize information into sequential packages. This creates difficulties for many learners because the approach is frequently one-dimensional. The brain learns best through rich, multi-dimensional, sensory experiences. Again, the question is not, How can I teach it best? but, How can my students learn it best?

Eric Jensen once asked us if we knew the difference between good teachers and exceptional teachers. Both, he said, reach 70 percent of their students. The good teacher reaches the same 70 percent all the time, while the exceptional teacher is reaching a different 70 percent at any given time. Even as challenged mathematicians, we know that the fewer ways we use to present information, the fewer chances we have of reaching all of our students. Each time we add a new action or way to present material, the probability of reaching more students increases.

At this point, some of you may be wondering if you have to have five different ways to present every lesson. The answer is no. What we try to do is match concepts with the most effective ways to present them. Sometimes we just stand and deliver the information, but we also use storytelling, drama, music, movement, visual aids (posters, overhead transparencies), videos, books, pictures, games, and manipulatives. When we use a conceptual, thematic approach in our teaching, one of the advantages we find is that we can get to the "big picture" in many different ways. Each of the activities we do as part of a theme contributes to students making meaning of the topic.

If one side of the learning coin is "presenting," the other side must be "representing." Just as we vary the ways we teach, we also provide students with a variety of ways to represent their learning so that they can construct their own meaning and understandings. The typical way to represent learning in school has been through writing. To begin expanding students' options, vary the way they respond in writing. For example, have them write a poem, a newspaper article, a list, a web, a mind-map, or a recipe. Once students have increased their repertoire of ways to represent through writing, they can go further by creating songs, stories, skits, and models. As teachers, we can encourage a broader scope of representation by providing students with time to think, access to supplies, support, and most of all, opportunities to share, discuss, reflect, and celebrate their representations. Providing time for students to share their representations gives them opportunities for recognition, for exchanging ideas, and for hearing and seeing new ways of thinking and looking at things. "Sharing time" is generative because students get ideas from one another. Sharing has an efficacious effect on students as they see how their work inspires their peers.

As teachers, we tend to teach in the ways that are most compatible to the ways we ourselves learn. Also, many of us teach the way we were taught. Unfortunately, that kind of thinking limits our ability to reach students who think and learn differently from us. Many educators have developed classification systems that help us consider learning styles and learning senses. Just as nutritionists use the food pyramid to help people plan a balanced diet, we can use these classification systems to ensure balance as we plan to meet the needs of our learners.

Classification Systems

- the five senses
- learning senses: VAK (visual, auditory, and kinesthetic)

- multiple intelligences
- learning domains (physical, social, emotional and cognitive, and aesthetic)

Each classification system gives us an opportunity to approach learning in a holistic way and also provides us with a reference so we can try to meet the needs of all learners. It does not matter which system you use; it matters that you have a system that works for you.

A multi-path approach to learning takes care of most of our learners. But it still is not enough. We need to provide enrichment for every learner who walks through our classroom doors. The ingredients necessary for enrichment are challenge, novelty, and feedback.

Judging the right amount of challenge is important. If there is too much, students may give up; if there is too little, they may get bored. We can provide challenge by introducing new material, increasing the degree of difficulty, adjusting the time allotted for activities, and/or limiting the resources.

As part of its survival response, the brain is constantly alert for anything novel in the environment. The reticular formation in our brain alerts us to what is new in the environment. Some educators refer to it as the "attention gate." As a situation becomes routine, the reticular formation is less active. When we do something new, it is alerted and we are more attentive.

The brain needs feedback. Feedback reduces stress because it reduces uncertainty. Feedback provides the information we need so we can decide what to do next. Feedback needs to be specific, timely, and continuous.

Brain-Body

The only exercise some people get is running out of money.

— Anonymous

We learn as a single integrated organism. What we do and how we feel are affected by our central nervous system, our immune system, and our peptide system. In our body, everything is connected. All learning is dependent on the body's physiological state. Renate Caine and Geoffrey Caine (1997a, 88), authors on learning and the brain, say, "The body is in the brain, and the brain is in the body. For most purposes, treating them as separate no longer makes sense." The nervous system is made up of the brain, the spinal cord, and millions of individualized nerve cells organized in bundles or cables. Recent research describes a second nervous system. Peptides, chains of amino acids found throughout the body, travel in the bloodstream and are the brain-body's primary source of information transfer. Eric Jensen (1998a, 57) says, "Another way of looking at it is, our entire body thinks, not just our brain."

Just as how the way we feel and what we eat affect our well-being, the amount of exercise we get affects our ability to remember and learn. Movement and learning have constant interplay. Exercise strengthens not only muscles, it effects the cerebellum and the corpus callosum in our brain. Our body takes cues from our mind, and conversely, our mind informs our body. Physical health and mental health have direct effects on how well our immune system functions. Illness and lack of sleep lower our capacity for attention. Sleep is necessary for the brain to process the day's events and build complex memories.

Frequent physical breaks are a requirement for every type of learning situation. By working our body, we prepare our brain to respond to challenges. The increased blood flow created by exercise results in more oxygen getting to the brain. Through movement we can reduce stress, improve short-term memory, help our neurons communicate better, decrease reaction time, and become more creative. Movement is not a luxury; it is a necessity.

Swinging, rolling, jumping, and playing games stimulate the inner ear and cerebellum, triggering the reticular formation. This formation of nuclei, located near the top of the brain stem, is critical for attention because it regulates information coming from our senses. This process affects our balance, coordination, and ability to turn thinking into action. The cerebellum, which affects posture, coordination, and movement, is also connected to the parts of the brain involved in memory, attention, and spatial perception. Physical education, movement, and games are important not only for good learning, but because they are fun. There is a direct link between the cerebellum and the emotional system. Having fun is not trivial; it decreases stress and increases the function of the immune system.

Involvement in the arts requires moving and doing, and provides further opportunities to integrate mind and body. While the connection to dance, drama, role-playing, and creative movement is obvious, the visual arts also help students develop visual thinking, problem-solving abilities, facility with language, and creativity. Music promotes relaxation, reduces stress, stimulates thinking, and is a brain-building block for math, science, and reading. In his article, "Art for the Brain Sake," Robert Sylwester (1998) says, "This discussion of the arts began with the importance of motion, and it ends with the importance of *emotion*. Both are central to the arts and to life."

Alcohol and tobacco have toxic effects on the body. Alcohol can reduce the brain's ability to remember and make connections. Pierce Howard (1999, 82) says, "Alcohol destroys the brain cells, primarily in the left hemisphere, the seat of language and logic." Howard also points out (1999, 86-87) that the interruption of the flow of oxygen to the brain caused by taking in nicotine decreases the metabolism of glucose, resulting in sluggish or faulty memory and less effective problem solving. Some researches have documented the negative effects certain food additives and chemicals have on the body. We need to give our students sufficient information so they can make wise and informed lifestyle choices.

Nearly everything we do and nearly all decisions we make are affected by the state we are in at the time. Some positive states are challenge, curiosity, anticipation, and self-convincing. Some less positive states are frustration, apathy, and fear. In his seminars, Eric Jensen says, "States are simply the mind-body moment made up of your thoughts and your physiology." Good teachers are good state-managers—they are able to read and manage states and can get their students into "managed" states for learning.

The time to ask your teenager to take out the garbage is not when he is lying on the couch, enjoying a television program or a good book. He is not in an appropriate state. The best time is as he is walking through the kitchen to get another bowl of ice cream.

As teachers, we need to give directions in a state that will induce activity ("Hey, I've got a great idea. Put your things down, please stand up, and..."). This kind of direction puts people into a state of anticipation. There are other ways to change states in our classrooms—playing music, role-playing, storytelling, standing up and moving about, sharing, getting food and water, listening to guest speakers, planning field trips, using humor, taking deep breaths, mind mapping, stretching, and getting and giving massages.

Routines or rituals in our classrooms provide great opportunities to put our students into good, common states. We have learned to evaluate the effect of the rituals we use in our classrooms to ensure that they promote positive states. One of our favorite rituals in Eric Jensen's seminar is something he calls GLP. Every day after lunch, we would return to class and then walk with someone to discuss three things: something we were grateful for (G), something we learned (L), and something we had promised (P). Every participant returned from the "GLP walk" energized (because of the movement) and motivated to get going on the afternoon's program (because of talking and the opportunity to make personal connections). We often use this same strategy with our students and with workshop participants so that they are in a positive state for learning.

Memory

Our memories are the fragile but powerful products of what
we recall from the past, believe about the
present, and imagine about the future.

— Daniel L. Schacter, *Searching for Memory*

Our brain does not store memories of whole events; it recreates them. Our memories are not neatly packaged miniature videotapes; they are engrams that, when activated, come together to allow us to recall information and experiences. The aspect of memory that is of greatest interest to most people is retrieval. Memory and retrieval cannot be separated. "Memory is determined by what kind of retrieval is activated" (Jensen 1998b, 102). There are pathways for specific types of learning and some types of memory are easier to retrieve than others. It is better to think of memory in terms of a process rather than in terms of a specific location.

Memories are often described as explicit and implicit. Explicit memory is further categorized as semantic and episodic; implicit memory is categorized as procedural and reflexive. Marilee Sprenger (1998) wrote about each of these categories as lanes of memory. Semantic memory deals with words and symbols, while episodic memory deals with time and space. The hippocampus is the structure in the brain that sorts and files semantic and episodic memory. Automatic, or "stimulus

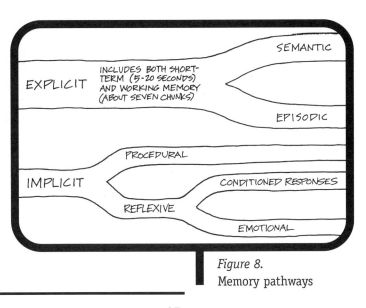

Figure 8.
Memory pathways

response" memory, and procedural, or "how to" memory, are centered in the cerebellum. Physical, procedural memories are sometimes called "muscle memories." Procedural memories are formed by doing and fixing through practice. The saying, "Hands on, minds on," describes active learning of procedural memory. Reflexive memory, also located in the cerebellum, refers to the things we do automatically like rote counting, saying the alphabet, and pulling a hand away from something hot.

Our strongest memories are processed by the amygdala, a structure in our forebrain. The amygdala filters information for emotional content, and catalogs and fixes our memories. The peptide molecules, circulating in our blood stream, also store and transfer information. Memory does not just happen in our brain, our whole body is involved in "remembering."

We receive and retrieve information through the same pathways. We need to chunk semantic information into small segments for easier recall. Acronyms, acrostics, pegging systems, mnemonic devices, mind maps, and graphic organizers can be effective ways to trigger recall of semantic memories. We can trigger episodic memories by returning to the location where the information was first learned. We have all experienced this type of memory: We might be in the living room and remember a phone call we need to make. We walk to the room where the phone is, forget why we are there, and then walk back into the living room to trigger the memory of the phone call.

In classrooms, we can help students remember by deliberately teaching in one place and assessing in the same place. Moving around the room or the school building to teach specific concepts is another way to promote episodic recall. We need to encourage students to make use of their episodic memory by reminding them to think of where they were when they were learning a concept. Our friend Trevor Calkins picks a spot in the classroom to teach long division, then reminds the students at a later date, "Remember when we were working on long division in the back corner of the room..." The best way to activate procedural memory is through physical movement. Reflexive memories depend on practice. Skills become automatic when they are "overlearned" through activities such as raps and games. Emotions enhance memory.

The way we set things up in our classrooms can help or hinder our students' memories. Our trick as teachers is to engage our students and then give them opportunities and time to make connections and establish memories.

Nutrition

It is becoming clearer that our brain influences what and how we eat, and that what and how we eat influences how we think and feel.

— Pierce J. Howard, *The Owner's Manual for the Brain*

As teachers, we do not have a lot of control over what our students eat. What we can do is give them information about nutrition. One of the most annoying things about studying the brain is that you find out your mother was right! Those "motherisms"—"drink eight glasses of water a day" and "eat your vegetables"—really *are* true. Studies of the effects of nutrition have demonstrated a strong correlation between the quantity of water we drink and quality of food we eat and how we feel and perform.

One of the immediate changes we made in our classrooms after our first seminar on brain-based learning was to invite students to bring water bottles to school. Dehydration, a common problem in the classroom, is linked to poor learning. By the time we are thirsty, we are already dehydrated. When that happens, we become less attentive and more lethargic. Water makes up over 70 percent of our brain. With thirst, the percentage of water in the blood goes down while the salt concentration in the blood goes up, causing rises in blood pressure and stress levels. If we become dehydrated, the chemical balance in our brain is negatively altered. Caffeine—found in coffee and tea, chocolate, and some carbonated beverages—is a diuretic and triggers the removal of water from the body. For better learning, it is important for teachers to help students understand the value of drinking water.

We cannot dictate what our students' food habits are, but we can give them information and help them learn which foods have positive effects on thinking, memory, learning, and well-being. A balanced diet of leafy green vegetables, fresh fruit, fish, lean meats, nuts, grains, and dairy products is ideal.

We learned about the relationship between food and the production of neurotransmitters in our brain. When we talk about neurotransmitters, we compare them to the way gas and brake pedals work in a car. The gas pedal is for speeding up; the brake is for slowing down. Different neurotransmitters in the brain either speed up or slow down our actions and thoughts.

Dopamine, norepinephrine, and serotonin are three chemicals manufactured in our brain. Dopamine, the pleasure and reward chemical, and norepinephrine help to keep us alert. Norepinephrine helps us think, react quickly and express ourselves, and boosts our motivation. It helps activate the body's "flight or fight" response. Serotonin has a calming effect. Its main purpose is to relax the central nervous system, giving a sense of well-being and self-confidence.

As we learned more about the chemicals in our brain, we became more intentional about what we ate. Eating a high-protein meal, like meat and legumes, supplies tyrosine, the nutrient the brain needs to manufacture dopamine and norepinephrine, essential for alertness and quick-thinking. Eating turkey and carbohydrates (like bread and pasta) supplies tryptophan, which is converted to serotonin in the brain. Serotonin makes us feel calm and more able to sleep. Choline-rich foods, like soybeans and eggs, boost levels of the neurotransmitter acetylcholine, necessary for memory and smooth muscle movement. Dairy products such as yogurt and milk supply the brain with calpain. Calpain is derived from calcium. It cleans the synapses by dissolving protein buildup, making the synapses more efficient for neural transmission.

We try to help our students understand how eating good food will improve performance, increase concentration, and boost energy by naturally altering or enhancing brain chemistry.

Cycles and Rhythms

You can either have your learners' attention or they can be making meaning for themselves, but not both at the same time.

— Eric Jensen

Stop bragging about getting your students' attention and keeping it for prolonged periods of time. Our brains are designed for ups and downs, not constant attention. Our bodies run in cycles, affected by breathing and energy levels. When we are at the top of our 90–110 minute cycle, we can pay better attention. When we are at the bottom of our cycle, our learning drops because we have less energy and less ability to pay attention.

Just as our body has cycles when we are awake, we have cycles when we are asleep. The sleep time vital for learning is the REM (rapid eye movement or dream state). REM is thought to be critical for retaining our memories. During REM sleep, the amygdala processes intense emotions and the hippocampus "sorts" memories, which the cortex then processes. During sleep, learning is consolidated. If we are deprived of sleep, our ability to recall complicated and complex material may be impaired. We have no more control over how much sleep our students get than we do over the quality of the food they eat. We can, however, build in rest times during the day. We can also take care of ourselves by catnapping (sorry, not during class time) as a way to stay alert. Einstein took short naps during the day. Many companies now encourage their workers to take twenty-minute power naps because this makes their employees more productive.

Our body chemistry, our emotions, and our diet continually trigger variations in the way we attend, remember, and learn. Saying a student is "on" or "off" task is immaterial because the brain is constantly attending to its need for survival, challenge, and rest. In the past, we worried about kids who did not constantly pay attention, and often labeled them as "problems." We put a lot of energy into getting and keeping everyone's attention by using bribes, rewards, punishments, threats, and gimmicks. These tricks may have given us a feeling of control and worked to "manage" our students, but they did not help students learn.

As educators, we cannot determine the stages and cycles of our students. However, we can provide choice and variety in an attempt to best achieve a productive learning climate for all. One way to alter the downside of the learner cycle is to use energizers, or physical breaks. We can also positively affect cycles through emotional engagements such as storytelling, singing, humor, drama, and games. Another way to respond to the needs of our learners is to plan large blocks of time for activities, and to give breaks and opportunities for students to be attentive, to interact, and to make meaning. The time we build in for our students to internalize personal understanding through reflection is not only valuable, it is a necessity. Downtime is essential if learners are to make neural connections. Neural fixing only happens when there are no competing stimuli, so we need to give students quiet, restful time and space. Even though we have learned to give blocks of time for processing, we know that it may take up to six hours for any skill or action to be imprinted. Our students may be making meaning when we least expect it.

> *In order to either proceed or figure it all out, a student must "go internal" and give up that "external" attention.*
>
> **—Eric Jensen, *Teaching With the Brain in Mind***

A practical way of dealing with the reality of biorhythms is to accept that cycles do happen. When we understand the cycles of energy and attention, we know that the notion of "getting students' attention and keeping it" is not productive.

Elimination of Threat

Creating a brain-compatible ambiance calls for deliberately identifying and stripping away sources of threat.

— Leslie A. Hart, *Human Brain and Human Learning*

Eric Jensen suggests we need to distinguish among stress, distress, and threat. Threat is caused when we feel defensive or helpless, giving the perception that our survival is at risk. This is bad for learning. Distress, also bad for learning, occurs when we are faced with multiple or uncontrollable stressors. Stress is a possible reaction to threat. The brain perceives a little stress as challenge; as long as the learner feels in control, stress can be good for learning. However, when we lose control of the stress, it becomes hazardous to learning. Distress and threat are the biggest contributors to impaired learning. The brain's priority is survival and when threatened the brain moves into survival mode at the expense of higher-order thinking skills. When it perceives danger—physical, academic, environmental, social, or emotional—the brain releases epinephrine, which prepares the body for "fight or flight." The adrenal glands release the peptide, cortisol. High cortisol levels over time lead to the death of brain cells in the hippocampus, impairing memory formation. The physical reactions to distress and threat are a suppressed immune system, tense large muscles, increase in blood pressure, and blood clotting. Chronically distressed people have trouble sorting out what is important and what is not. Distress and threat create a vicious cycle of underachievement that can lead to illness and disengagement, which then lead back to poor achievement.

Under distress and threat, the blood flow and electrical activity in the brain are concentrated in the brain stem and cerebellum and decreased in the midbrain and cortex. Leslie Hart (1983) calls this "downshifting." Jensen (1996) prefers the term "survivalized." He points out that all areas of the brain are still being used, but to a lesser degree. When the brain goes into survival mode, it tends to revert to instinct, becomes more automatic, is less able to take clues from the environment, and is less able to perceive relationships and patterns. When we feel overstressed and threatened, we are less able to solve problems.

Brain-Based Learning With Class

For students, threat and distress can come from many sources: fear of physical harm from classmates, staff, family, or others; time pressures and lack of resources; cultural and social disrespect; intellectual intimidations; and emotional jeopardy. Poor physical conditions such as overcrowding and inadequate lighting add to stress. Expecting all students to perform well in highly stressful classrooms is unrealistic. For example, under stress, it is difficult for students to track a page of print or stay focused on a small area of print because the eyes become more attentive to peripheral areas, scanning for danger. We cannot always be sure what the stessors are for individual students, but we can be observant, we can listen, and we can try to establish a safe, supportive atmosphere.

Rewards are one source of stress that many educators provide with the best intentions. They do not realize that the anxiety of rewards can trigger the release of neurotransmitters that may inhibit creativity, problem solving, and recall. Those who are rewarded may become stressed with the pressure of having to repeat accomplishments. The flip side of rewards is punishment for those who do not receive a reward.

Rather than risk the threat associated with rewards, we take every opportunity to celebrate and help students recognize their own achievements. In *Recognition Without Rewards,* Cameron et al. provide practical suggestions for encouraging all learners. We try to create communities of learners who support and respect one another. We use structures such as collaborative grouping to help students work together, and we avoid systems such as homogenous grouping, which stress students by labeling them.

Students considered to be at-risk live in a constant state of threat. They tend to make biologically driven choices, do what works, aim for short-term goals, watch their backs, and are generally unmotivated. Under the constant stress, the parietal and frontal lobes receive less blood; thinking is more literal.

Research shows that threatening students and putting them in stressful situations can impair brain cells and change the body's chemistry negatively. We must try to identify the sources of stress and threat in our classrooms and avoid or reduce them. As teachers, we can be the source of stress or we can create a nonthreatening environment.

PART TWO

Teaching About the Brain

In this section, we provide educators with suggestions and activities for teaching students about the brain. When we first became interested in brain-based learning, and when we thought about teaching our students about the brain, we wondered how we could add yet another topic to our already crammed curriculum. After we learned even more about brain-based learning, we wondered, How can we *not* teach our students about how their brain works and how they learn?

Since we have started doing a brain theme in our classrooms, we have seen the benefits unfold through all other curricular areas and units of study. By teaching our students about the brain, we have helped them learn about themselves: what kinds of learners they are, how they can help themselves become better learners, and how they can deal with their emotions in positive ways.

CHAPTER FOUR

Doing Brain Basics With Class

When our students discover the wonders of how their brains work, not only are they amazed and appreciative, they also gain a new language of learning. A classroom where students talk about the way they make connections, the effect of practice on myelination (see page 11), and strategies for problem solving is a delight to be in! Learning about the brain has helped our students do their best and be their best.

When we study the brain, we usually follow this sequence:

- Getting Started: WIIFM

- Getting Started: SWYAK

- How Is Your Brain Like...?

- Mapping the Brain

- Making a Model of the Brain

- The Learning Connection

- Introducing the Brain Basics With Class

- Unpacking the Brain Basics

- Celebrating Brain-Based Learning

The amount of time you spend and the depth you go into with the activities will depend on the ages and interests of your students and your personal commitment.

Getting Started: WIIFM

Just as we asked you to begin your own study of the brain by asking the WIIFM question, you should involve your students in this same process.

When students feel that an activity is purposeful and worth their time and effort, they are more likely to be motivated and actively involved. Sometimes relevance is easy to see; other times it takes some searching and imagination.

Activity: What's In It For Me? (WIIFM)

Why

To establish personal relevance and purpose

How

Note: Whenever we introduce an activity in this book, we say, "Talk with students..." What we mean is this: Get the conversation going, then step back and allow students their voices. You will find your students have lots to say.

- Talk with students about why it might be worth their time to learn about the brain.

- Give the students time to share their ideas with others.

- Share and brainstorm (to trigger connections) with large groups.

- Have students record their personal WIIFM.

- Allow students time to go back during and after a unit of study to check their WIIFM.

Learning Link: How can I adapt this activity?

_____

_____

Getting Started: SWYAK

We learn best when we make personal connections to what we already know. Every learner is unique and has prior knowledge. We need to recognize this experience base and help our students build on it. We cannot intuitively know how much each of our students already knows or how each feels about a topic. The best way to help students make learning meaningful is by having them show what they already know.

Have students use meaning and memory maps, posters, drawings, diagrams, lists, or other ways of representing. These representations become the baseline or launching pad for exploring concepts. Throughout the unit or theme, students will return to their original pieces and add or revise them as their knowledge grows. Whether you are studying the brain, division, the life cycle of a butterfly, or Shakespeare, SWYAK is a worthwhile and necessary beginning.

> *Students who do not have much prior knowledge of a topic need to be paired with someone who does. They also need to be actively involved so they can develop an experience base.*

Activity: Show What You Already Know (SWYAK)

Why

To establish prior knowledge

How

- Talk with students about the importance of recording what they already know as a way to make connections with new learning.

- Demonstrate ways to record (for example, webbing, list, meaning and memory map, diagrams).

- Have students work individually or in small groups.

- Ask students to talk about and record what they already know about the brain.

- Give students an opportunity to share and add to their representations (see Browse, Borrow, and Build, page 75, and Museum Walkabout, page 86).

- Have students add to their SWYAK pages several times during the theme—we call this activity Show What You Know Now (SWYKN).

Learning Link: How can I adapt this activity?

_____

_____

How Is Your Brain Like...?

Talk with students about the value of making connections as a way to understand new information. When we understand some of the ways we learn, we can use this knowledge to be better learners. This is why we teach our students about learning connections. Once we have taught this concept, we are amazed at the enthusiasm and ability of our students to apply it to their learning.

Why

To help students make connections

How

- Talk with students about the value of making connections as a way to understand new information.

- Collect a walnut, a cabbage, raisins, a pillowcase or a page from a newspaper, a grapefruit, an avocado or a bowl of porridge, and some string cheese.

- Show students the items that make us think about different parts of the brain.

- Send a sheet home that lists the items. Ask students to talk with their families and record what connections they can make between the things on the list and what they speculate or already know about the brain.

- In the classroom, put each item on a table top at a different station around the room. Include a large piece of chart paper at each station. Divide the class into groups and, in their groups, have the students record their ideas at each station.

- Tell students that when they are finished, they will meet together so they can share what they have written.

- Tell them how their comments match with the information that is known about the brain (see page 41).

Date _____   Name _____

How is your brain like...?

a cabbage
a raisin
a pillowcase
a grapefruit
an avocado/porridge
string cheese
a walnut

Figure 9.
How is your
brain like...?
(Reproducible master
in appendix)

How is your brain like a cabbage?

The weight of the brain is approximately the same weight as a medium-sized cabbage (about 1350 g or 3 lb.). Our young students like to carry the cabbage around (until it starts to smell!) by holding it like a waiter's tray. They get a sense of the weight of their head on their body. Students usually mention that both the cabbage and the brain have a stem.

How is your brain like a raisin?

The brain and the raisin are both wrinkled, or convoluted. One of our favorite responses to this question came from a six-year-old student who said, "I know that my brain was the size of a raisin when I was in my mom's tummy!"

How is your brain like a pillowcase?

If our brain was not wrinkled, or convoluted, it would be approximately the same size as a pillowcase. Some suggest it is about the same size as an unfolded sheet of newspaper. We point out that if the brain were not convoluted, our heads would be very large and birthing would be difficult. One student asked Colleen, "What about hammerhead sharks?"

How is your brain like a grapefruit?

The skin of a grapefruit is approximately the same thickness as the cortex. Knowledgeable participants in workshops often make the comparison that the grapefruit, like the brain, consists of a high percentage of water.

How is your brain like an avocado?

The consistency and texture of a ripe avocado is similar to the texture of the brain. We sometimes use cooked porridge for this connection, if an avocado is unavailable. We often use this demonstration as an opportunity to talk about how neurosurgeons use suctioning devices rather than scalpels when operating on the brain.

How is your brain like string cheese?

The corpus callosum is the bundle of axons that links the two halves of the brain. We fan out the string cheese to show the fibers, telling students that the fibers in the corpus callosum are even finer than a strand of hair.

When we have finished this activity, we challenge our students to find other objects they can use to make connections to what they are learning about the brain. One of our favorites is a hairnet. When placed on an overhead projector surface, the hairnet looks like connections inside the brain.

How is your brain like a walnut?

The function of a walnut shell is similar to the function of the skull. It protects what is inside. Students often point out that the walnut has two sides, like the brain.

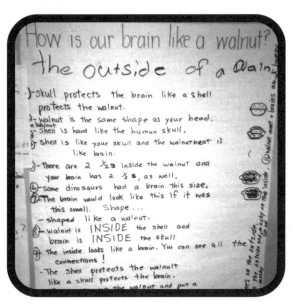

If you want to emphasize the importance of a protective shell, bring a hard-boiled egg to the class. You can create a dramatic moment by dropping the egg on the floor as you are talking. This is guaranteed to turn the conversation to how fragile the brain is and the need for protective helmets when riding a bicycle, playing hockey, and so on.

Whenever we can, we bring in a brain specimen to show to our students. So far we have had a brain from a deer, a pig, and a salmon. Colleen tells her students that words like *yuck, gross,* and *ugh* are not scientific terms (a message the students carry to their parents).

Mapping the Brain

When we introduce students to the parts of the brain, we begin by mapping an apple.

Activity: Mapping an Apple

Why

To help students think about components of the brain from different perspectives

How

- Talk with students about different ways to look at an object.

- Show the students an apple.

- Ask them to describe what they can see from the outside of the apple.

- Cut the apple in half horizontally and ask students to describe what they can see.

- Cut the apple in half vertically and ask students to describe what they can see.

- Draw a map of the apple on an overhead transparency or on chart paper.

- Ask students what connections they can make between the apple and what they already know about the brain. (We often hear: the apple has a stem, the brain has a stem; you cut the apple into four pieces, the brain has four lobes; the inside of the apple has parts you cannot see from the outside, just like the brain.)

Learning Link: How can I adapt this activity?

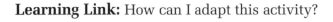

Activity: Mapping the Brain

Another way to introduce students to mapping the brain is to use the analogy of a trip to a mall or park. When we go to a mall or park we are familiar with, we often go to the same places to shop or to play. We have no trouble getting there because we know where those places are. If we were at a new mall or park, however, we would likely consult a map or directory. When we are learning about a new topic such as the brain, it helps to have a map to follow.

Why

To help students learn the names of the parts of the brain

How

- Talk with students about building their knowledge of the brain by learning where the parts are located.

- Show a map of a local park, mall, amusement center, or your school and talk about what information the map gives you.

- Reproduce figure 1 and figure 2 (see appendix), which show the right and left hemispheres and the four lobes of the brain, as sheets for students or as overhead transparencies. Talk about the function of the hemispheres and the four lobes (see pages 7–8).

- Reproduce and show figure 3 (see appendix), which shows the "outside-in" view of the brain, and describe the functions (see page 8).

- Continue by showing figure 4, the midbrain region, and figure 5, the lower brain (see appendix), and describe their functions (see pages 8–9).

The detail you go into and the time you take to teach this material will depend on the ages, abilities, and interest of your students.

Learning Link: How can I adapt this activity?

_____

_____

Making a Model of the Brain

Making a model helps students get a visual and kinesthetic sense of an abstract concept. It also gives them a way to demonstrate or represent what they have learned, and provides educators with insights into students' understanding.

Activity: Making a Model of the Brain

Why

To help students demonstrate knowledge of their "brain geography"

How

■ Talk with students and remind them that we started investigating the brain by looking at a three-dimensional object (apple) and learned how it could be represented on a flat map. Tell students one of the ways they can show what they have learned from looking at and talking about the brain maps is to make a three-dimensional model.

■ Brainstorm with students possibilities for models and make a list of materials needed. (Our students have made models from headbands, hats, Plasticine, Play-Doh, and even Lego.)

■ When the models are complete, have students label and display their work.

■ Give each student an opportunity to describe what his or her model illustrates about the brain.

Learning Link: How can I adapt this activity?

_____

_____

The Learning Connection

Neurons are one of two types of cells in our brain. Each neuron is made up of a cell body with multiple branches called dendrites and one long extension called an axon. Neurons communicate with one another in a cell-to-cell process. Electrical impulses trigger the release of neurotransmitters located at the ends of the axon. These neurotransmitters are absorbed by receptor sites at the end of dendrites, which then make it possible for the impulse to bridge the gap or synapse between neurons.

Activity: Knowing Neurons

Why

To help students learn about neurons

How

■ Talk with students about how interesting and valuable it is for them to understand how their brain makes connections.

- Ask students to hold one hand in the air with their fingers spread out.

- Using your hand as a model, point to your palm and say, "This part of my hand represents the cell body of a neuron." Wiggle your fingers and say, "The fingers of my hand represent the dendrites that branch from each neuron. My hand has five digits but mature neurons have many more dendrites." Run your fingers down your arm and say, "My arm represents the axon, which extends from each neuron."

- Have students turn to a partner and use their hand to practice naming the parts of the neuron.

- Use figure 6 (see appendix) as a chart or overhead transparency to review the parts of the neuron (see page 11).

Activity: Communicating Neurons

Why

To introduce students to the process of neural communication

How

- Talk with students about how interesting and valuable it is to understand how our brain makes connections.

- Show students figure 6 (see appendix) as a chart or overhead transparency to review the parts of the neuron.

- Say, "At baseball games, fans sometimes do a wave by raising their arms, one after the other, in the air. The wave travels from one end of the row to the other and then on to the next row. This is similar to the way messages travel down neurons. But instead of arms being thrown in the air, pulses of electricity are fired off one after another, traveling from one axon to the next." Do the wave with your students to demonstrate the action.

- Show figure 7 (see appendix) as an overhead transparency. Explain, "This diagram shows two neurons. When neurons communicate, an electrical impulse travels down the axon of one neuron toward the dendrite of another neuron. (Use a washable marker to show the path of the impulse.) The axon does not touch the dendrite because there is a gap called a synapse. The electrical impulse from the axon stimulates the release of chemicals stored in the receptors located at the end of the dendrite. If the right chemicals are present (excitatory), the signal jumps the gap and travels to the next neuron. If the wrong chemicals are present (inhibitory), the signal cannot jump the gap. There are fifty of these chemicals, called neurotransmitters. How much sleep we get, food we eat, water we drink, exercise we get, and how we feel (safe, happy, threatened, nervous, frightened) affect which neurotransmitters are released. The better we feel physically and mentally, the easier it is to learn." (Simply put, brain basics tell you this: if you are watered, well fed, happy, making meaning, and so on, excitatory chemicals will be present; if you are feeling threatened, inhibitory chemicals can block learning.)

■ Tell the students that when the same axon is used repeatedly, a white, fatty substance called myelin coats the axon, speeding up the cell-to-cell communication process. The most-used axons, or longer axons, are coated. Short axons are not myelinated because it would serve no purpose. Jensen (1998b, 12) says it would be like putting a freeway on a one-block side street. When learning to play the piano, we have to think about everything from reading the music to which fingers to move. As we practice, these things become automatic because sets of neurons are connected together to create shortcuts that speed up the thinking process. In her workshops, Pat Wolfe says, "Neurons that wire together, fire together!"

Activity: Making Neurons!

This activity is especially useful for visual and kinesthetic learners.

Why

To give students a hands-on opportunity to make a neuron model

How

■ Talk with students about the value of making models.

■ Review the previous activity.

■ Have students collect and bring Styrofoam plates or trays to school.

■ Have each student (or pair of students) make a "neuron," using a Styrofoam tray or dinner plate covered with plastic wrap and white school glue. Demonstrate by squeezing a small puddle of glue onto the center of the tray or plate. Use the lid of the bottle to pull out the glue to form an axon and dendrites. With a water-base felt pen, color the center of the glue neuron. Let dry overnight. The next morning, bend the tray or plastic wrap and peel to remove the neuron model. Put neurons on an overhead projector to display and discuss. Remind students that the process of myelination takes place on most long and well-used axons. Ask students which axons in their brains would most likely be myelinated and invite them to think of ways to show how this could look.

> *If you are working with older students, you may want to discuss and design activities to help them learn about the receptors found on the cell body and on the peptides, which circulate throughout the body.*

Introducing the Brain Basics With Class

Once your students know what the parts of the brain are and how the parts work together, it is time for them to think about how they can use this information to help them become even better learners. We tell our students that when we first started to learn about the brain, Eric Jensen, our teacher, gave us a list of ten important things to remember about learning. We have developed this list into our ten brain basics. Teach these ten brain basics to your students so that they can always remember ways to help themselves think and learn best.

One effective way to help recall a list of items is to use a "link and peg" system. Involve your students in learning a list of "pegs," then have them "link" each peg word with the words you want them to learn. Because the pegs are visual as well as semantic cues, students find them easy to remember. The list of pegs becomes a constant that is embedded in the memory. The list of items can be plugged into the peg list. For example, the number one word on the list is *sun* because there is one sun. Eric Jensen links this to the first principle, uniqueness, by saying, "There is one *u* in the word *sun*, and that stands for 'you' because you are unique!"

Activity: Pegging the Brain Basics

Why

To help recall the brain basics using a "link and peg" system

How

- Talk with students about how using a pegging system can help them to remember new information.

The Pegging System

#1: sun: There is only one sun.
#2: eyes, ears: We have two eyes and two ears.
#3: three pigs: In the story *The Three Little Pigs*, the pigs were happy, sad, and fearful.
#4: table: A table has four legs.
#5: five senses: We have five senses.
#6: sticks: Five, six, pick up sticks.
#7: telephone: There are seven digits in a telephone number.
#8: snowman: A snowman is shaped like the number eight.
#9: baseball: There are nine players on the field and nine innings in the game.
#10: countdown: Countdown for a blastoff!

Figure 10.
The pegging system
(Reproducible master in appendix)

- Teach the peg words 1–5. With each, explain why the peg word and the number match. (For example, "There is only one *u* in the word *sun*.")

- Have the students practice 1–5 with a partner.

- Teach the peg words 6–10. With each, explain why the word and the number match.

- Have the students practice 6–10 with a partner.

- Add the "link" word for each peg 1–5 (for example, unique is the link word for #1), explain the connection you are making, then have students practice 1–5.

  #1: sun: unique: There is only one *u* in the word *sun*, and only one you in the world.

  #2: eyes, ears: assessment: You use your eyes and ears to observe and collect information.

  #3: three pigs: emotions: The story, *The Three Little Pigs*, is full of emotions—happiness, sadness, and fear.

  #4: table: meaning: There are four legs on a table and you have meaningful conversation around a table.

  #5: five senses: multi-path: Your senses provide you with information.

- Add the "link" word for each peg 6–10, explain the connection you are making, then have students practice 6–10.

  #6: sticks: brain-body: You use your brain to count the sticks and your body to pick up the sticks.

  #7: telephone: memory: There are seven digits to remember in a telephone number.

  #8: snowman: nutrition: Feed the snowman; the snowman is made out of water.

  #9: baseball: cycles and rhythms: In baseball, there are nine innings and nine players.

  #10: countdown: elimination of threat: Countdown for a blastoff!

Learning Link: How can I adapt this activity?

_____

_____

Brain-Based Learning With Class

Unpacking the Brain Basics

Once students have mastered the list and their links, "unpack" or teach the students about each of the brain basics. In the following pages, we include the main ideas we talk about with our primary students. When we unpack the brain basics, we usually do the first five in one session and the next five at another session. We often talk about the brain basics in our classrooms, so that each of the concepts becomes part of daily practice. How much detail you share with your students will depend on their prior knowledge, ages, and interest. If you teach older students, you might want to refer back to the material we provided in chapter 3, Introducing the Brain Basics (see pages 15–33), consult other references, or have your students research the brain basics.

#1: sun: unique: There is only one *u* in the word *sun*, and only one you in the world.

- Just as everyone in the world has his or her own unique fingerprints, everyone has a unique brain.

- We each have different genetics and different experiences, and live and work in different environments, which is why we think and act in our own way.

- We each have different, equally valuable strengths, ways, and styles of learning. (Just because you have a different way of thinking or doing things does not mean your way is wrong. It is just the way you think and learn best.)

- We each develop at a different rate. For example, some people can ride a two-wheeler when they are three; others cannot ride a two-wheeler until they are nine.

- Boys and girls are different partly because there are differences in their brains.

#2: eyes, ears: assessment: We use our eyes and ears to observe and collect information.

- We use our eyes and ears to watch and listen for new experiences so we can learn.

- We use our eyes to help us make judgments about the work we do, and we use our ears to listen to the ideas of others.

- We can use what we learn from watching and listening to others to help ourselves become better learners.

- When we learn to use our own eyes and ears to look at and think about our own work, we learn what quality is for us. We can help ourselves instead of relying on the opinion of others.

#3: three pigs: emotions: The story, *The Three Little Pigs*, is full of emotions—happiness, sadness, and fear.

- The way we feel (happy, sad, worried, scared, angry, delighted) affects how well we can think. If we worry about something, it takes most of our brain's attention and we do not have that attention to pay to our learning. When we feel happy and secure, learning is easier.

- We can help ourselves deal with bad feelings by talking about them, by doing some kind of exercise, or by getting involved in an activity we like.

- Sometimes we can feel bad and we do not know why we feel like we do. We do not have to let that feeling ruin our learning or our day. We might talk to someone, or do something to help us get into a better state for learning. Sometimes, we just need some quiet time to figure it out.

#4: table: meaning: There are four legs on a table and we have meaningful conversation around a table.

- If something does not make sense to us, it can never have any meaning. If something has no meaning, we can never learn or remember it. If something does not make sense to us, it is our responsibility to get help or ask for a different explanation.

- When we learn something new, it is best if we can connect the new learning with something we already know. When we have the big picture, it makes it easier to understand how things fit together.

- When we learn something new, it is best if we can think of how learning this would be useful to us (WIIFM). When we know WIIFM, we become more interested.

- We need to have time to make sense and reflect about what we are learning. We can turn and talk to someone, draw, map, write, or teach someone else.

#5: five senses: multi-path: Our senses provide us with information.

- We learn through all our senses.

- We each use some senses better than other senses. If we are having trouble learning something one way, we need to try to learn it another way. It is our responsibility to find the senses that work best for us. These are easiest for us, but we must remember to use the other senses to aid in our learning.

- The reason we do VAK (visual, auditory, kinesthetic) activities in class is so all students can get to know and use their strengths and are challenged to try things in new ways (see VAK activities, page 83).

- The reason we do things in novel ways is because the brain, as part of its survival, is always on the alert for things that are different.

#6: sticks: brain-body: We use our mind to count and our body to pick up the sticks.

- We do not think with just our brain; we think with our whole body.

- If we are feeling tired or having trouble focusing, we need to move our body to help our brain reconnect (try crossovers, Simon Says, or getting up and moving to another part of the room).

- We need to get enough sleep so that our brain can do its nightly work of reviewing the day and then sort and file our memories.

- When people drink too much alcohol, they have trouble remembering.

- Smoking constricts the arteries that go to the brain; the brain then does not get as much oxygen and cannot work as well.

- Listening to music can reduce our stress, relax us, and help us think better.

- When we draw, paint, sculpt, dance, tell stories, and act, our mind and body work together.

#7: telephone: memory: There are seven digits to remember in a telephone number.

- There are different ways of remembering. Sometimes we remember things by remembering where we were at the time; sometimes we remember things because we have practiced them over and over again; sometimes we remember things because they made us feel happy or sad.

- Our memories are not like little videotapes playing in our brain. Every time we remember something, our brain recreates the memory from all the bits and pieces it has stored. (For example, when we think of cookies we might remember the feel of the cookie dough on our hands, the smell of the cookies as they bake, the taste of the warm cookie, and the good feelings we got when others tasted the cookies and liked them!)

- Most people can remember seven things, plus or minus two (for example, telephone numbers); it is easier to remember when we chunk things together.

- We can remember things through rhymes, acrostics, pegging systems, mind-mapping, retelling, and recalling where we were when we first learned something.

- How well we remember something depends on how we were feeling when we first learned it and how interested we were in what was going on.

#8: snowman: nutrition: Feed the snowman; the snowman is made out of water.

- Water makes up over 70 percent of our brain so it is important for us to keep the water and the chemicals in our brain balanced— drink lots of water (always keep a water bottle handy). By the time we are thirsty, our body is already dehydrated.

- We need to eat food from all the food groups so that our body can give our brain the nutrients it needs to perform well.

- We need to eat protein because our brain needs protein to do its best thinking.

- Foods like bread and pasta help to make us calm.

- We need milk and yogurt because they produce calpain, which helps to clean our synapses.

#9: baseball: cycles and rhythms: In baseball, there are nine innings and nine players.

- Sometimes we can pay attention and sometimes it is hard for us to pay attention because our body and brain work in cycles. We are more alert for some parts of the cycle; for other parts of the cycle we are less energetic.

- Even when it seems like we are not paying attention, our brain is active—it is just paying attention to something else.

- When we are feeling sluggish, we can help ourselves by moving around, getting a drink, having a catnap, or doing something in a different way.

- The state we are in depends on the way we are thinking and feeling. Everything we do is affected by the state we are in; sometimes the state we are in is not a good state for learning. What we choose to do can put us in a better state for learning.

- In the classroom, we can plan breaks and movement activities to help raise energy levels.

#10: countdown: elimination of threat: Countdown for a blastoff!

- When we are feeling threatened, our brain does not work as well and we tend to react rather than think things through. When we are worried or afraid, our brain is focused on survival and we do not do as good a job of solving problems. If we feel threatened, we need to use strategies to help calm us and get our good thinking back.

- When we feel upset, angry, frightened, or threatened, our large muscles tense and our eyes scan for danger; it is hard for us to focus on small areas like a page of print or a sheet of paper. We need to take time to walk around, loosen up, and relax our muscles before we try to do a job that requires close attention.

- When things at home or school make us feel threatened, it can interfere with our thinking. We can learn strategies to help us cope—talk to someone, practice the elevator strategy (see page 120), count to ten, or move to a different place in the room.

Celebrating Brain-Based Learning

When we do the brain theme with our students, we find that the information we learned about the brain becomes part of the everyday language and life in our classrooms. With all theme or concept studies, there comes a time when students need to have a new focus for learning. We like to end a theme with a celebration.

We have three main ways to tie a theme together. "Tying together" a theme is necessary because it helps us recognize and appreciate the learning that has taken place. We give students opportunitites to celebrate what they have learned by:

1. involving them in activities that let them talk about their learning.

2. inviting them to make products.

3. encouraging them to do demonstrations to represent their learning.

Some ways we like to wrap up the brain theme are:

■ talking: one-minute speeches, countdown of top ten favorite facts about the brain, commercials, brain jeopardy

■ products: posters, models, maps, banners, flags, letters, word searches, puzzles

■ demonstrations: open house, touring other classes, performances, displays, and a party to celebrate learning about the brain

PART THREE

Living the Brain Basics With Class

As experienced teachers, we instinctively know what works well with all learners. Many of the ideas and activities we discovered as we learned about the brain turned out to be the "classics" that have worked for years in our classrooms.

One of the greatest things about taking a brain-based approach is that you do not have to make huge changes in the way you already think or teach. Many teachers find that making small adaptations or taking baby steps can have dramatic results. We believe the change comes from learning why certain activities and approaches are consistently successful. It is this awareness that has helped us to become more intentional about creating the brain-based classroom.

What you will find in this section is not just a collection of activities, but a way of thinking about school. We have included activities for each of the brain basics. Again, we stress, adapt, not adopt, the activities to suit your style and your students' needs. The purpose for using these activities is to connect practice to theory. There are many possibilities for activities; we are just giving you some examples that work well for us. As you look through the activities, you will probably think of your own personal favorites to include in each category. That's great! Please send them to us to share with other "brain groupies!"

C H A P T E R   F I V E

Uniqueness Activities

*...learning actually changes the structure of the brain;
the more we learn, the more unique we become.*

—Caine and Caine, *Making Connections*

Activity: 4-Corner Reading/4-Corner Presentations

Why

To give students a chance to present to a small, interested audience, and to give the audience a choice of presentations

How

■ Talk with students about the value of presentations and choice.

■ Provide a sheet for students to sign up on when they are ready to read to a group or share information (see figure 11).

■ Give students an opportunity to prepare and rehearse. It is helpful to set a time limit for presenters at this point.

■ Meet as a whole group so that four students can introduce and "sell" their story or presentation. (For 4-Corner Reading, our students say things like, "If you like funny stories about big dogs, you'll want to come to my corner!" or "If you're interested in learning more about moon rocks, you'll want to come to my corner.")

■ Before they move to the corners, we divide the number of students in our class by four, determining how many spectators can go to each corner. We remind presenters of the time limit (usually ten minutes).

■ The students move to one of the four corners and the presentations begin.

Note: It usually takes a school week, plus one or two more days, to hear everyone in the class.

- When the time is up, the audience meets as a whole group. The presenters stand at the front so they can receive specific compliments and comments.

4 CORNER READERS/PRESENTERS

MONDAY	TUESDAY	WEDNESDAY	THURSDAY	FRIDAY
Paul Emma Alex Jaclyn	Tia Nicole Wey Ming Ravi	Davinder Kyra Amit Leon	Yuri Duncan Mica Bernie	Ben Rebecca John Sally

Figure 11.
4-corner
sign-up sheet

Learning Link: How can I adapt this activity?

_____

_____

Activity: Fan Letters

Why

To recognize and respect uniqueness

How

- Talk with students about why it is important to recognize and value each person's special qualities and talents.

- Distribute legal-size (22 cm x 36 cm; 8 1/2" x 14") paper and ask each student to fold a sheet into a fan (accordion folds).

- Have students put a name card at their place and leave their fan with their card.

- Have students move from place to place, look at the name, and then write a positive remark stating what they admire, respect, or have noticed about each classmate.

- Have students sign their comments, fold the paper down, and move onto the next fan until all the spaces on all the fans are filled.

- Have students return to their places and read their "fan letters."

Brain-Based Learning With Class

- Give students time to talk to one another about the comments on their letters.

Learning Link: How can I adapt this activity?

Activity: Strategy Wall

Why

To remind students that there are several ways they can respond to something (Joy's wall is a collection of literacy activities, but we have also seen math walls.)

How

- Talk with students about how posting strategies can help with decision making.

- Collect an example of student work for each strategy the class has done together.

- Label and display the sample of student work on the "strategy wall."

- Use the samples as a reminder of the choices students have when representing their thinking.

- Add to the wall each time a new strategy is introduced.

Learning Link: How can I adapt this activity?

Activity: 15-Second Spotlight

Why

To give all students an opportunity to share their opinion (students who rarely volunteer are encouraged to have a "short" turn, and students who never stop talking are reminded that their time is limited)

How

- Talk with students about the need to have activities that give all students a chance to be heard.

- Explain to students that it is important to hear a variety of views, opinions, and ways of saying things. Discuss how some students are shy about sharing with large groups and about how others take a long time to say something.

- Ask students to prepare what they are going to say and to remember to be clear and concise because they will have only fifteen seconds to speak.

- Ask two or three students to be timekeepers.

- Instead of going around the group one student after the other, use a nerf "brain" football to add some novelty to the activity. When one person has finished talking, he or she throws the football to someone else in the room. (Joy often has fifty students because she teams with another teacher, Fran Beckow, in a family grouping. Fifty students having a turn at one sitting takes too long—so they have three or four "spotlight sessions" throughout the day.)

    - Record key points, or ask two or three students to be the recorders. Display these points on a chart or bulletin board so that students can see what they have learned or what they know.

Learning Link: How can I adapt this activity?

_____

_____

Activity: Presentation Bingo

Why

To assist teachers in planning and evaluating a variety of teaching and learning strategies and activities to reach their students' uniqueness

How

- Use the presentation brain bingo sheet (see appendix), or design your own categories, to help you plan a variety of activities for a day, a series of lessons, a theme, or a unit of study. The bingo card has suggestions for ways to present material, and offers activities. Space is provided underneath each heading for you to write in specific references for your classroom.

- While working on a topic, mark the bingo card to check for balance in the types of activities and teaching methods you have used. If you are working on a topic for a day or a series of lessons, aim for a single line bingo. If you are working on a longer theme or unit, try to go for several lines, or even the ultimate—a blackout!

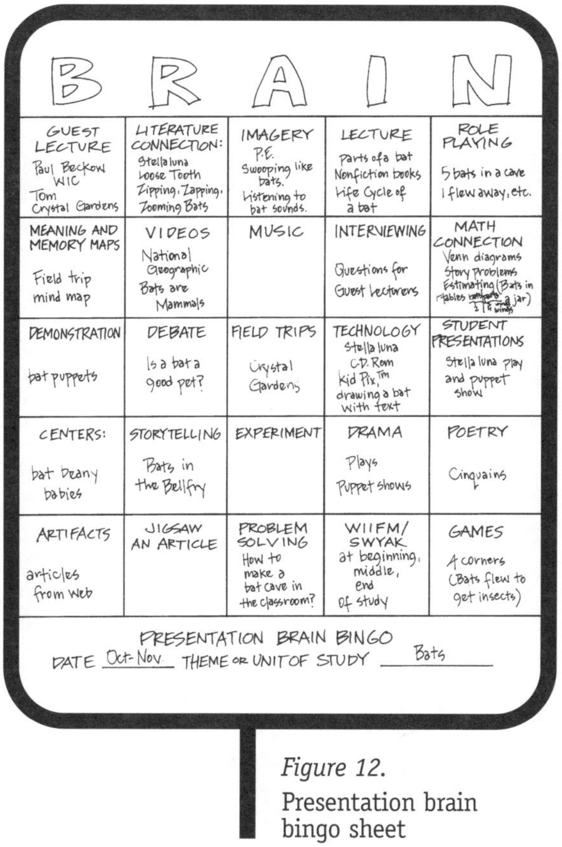

Learning Link: How can I adapt this activity?

_____

_____

Figure 12.
Presentation brain bingo sheet
(Reproducible master in appendix)

CHAPTER SIX

Assessment Activities

Evaluation should inform.
—Robert J. Anthony et al., *Evaluating Literacy*

Activity: Frequent Feedback

Why

To help students be successful by giving them ways to receive feedback that is timely, specific, and useful

How

- Talk with students about why it is important for them to know how they are doing. (Our students tell us, "It's important so you can do your best, so you don't keep making the same mistake, so you can set new goals, so you know you're on the right track, so you know when you need help, and so you know how to get better...")

- Say, "As your teacher, I try to give you helpful feedback as often as I can. But what's important is that you learn to look at what you do and judge it yourself. Sometimes you want another opinion and sometimes you need someone else's perspective. You can help yourself and you can help each other."

- Ask the students how they can get feedback from their classmates. Some suggestions are:

  - talk/discussion

  - comparison with a model

  - Specific Compliments (see page 66)

  - Compliment Chains (see page 70)

  - Browse, Borrow, and Build (see page 75)

  - 2 Hurrahs and a Hint (see page 64)

  - 2 Stars and a Wish (see page 64)

- applause

- written responses

- thumbs up

- setting and checking criteria

- celebratory music

- Quality Control (see page 65)

■ On a chart, list ways students can give one another feedback. Display the chart and ask the students which kinds of feedback they give to themselves and which kinds they can give to others.

Learning Link: How can I adapt this activity?

_____

_____

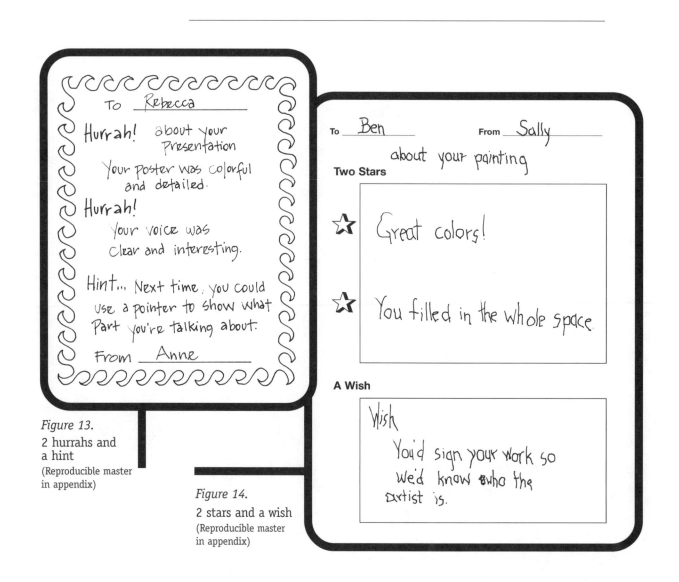

Figure 13.
2 hurrahs and
a hint
(Reproducible master
in appendix)

To ___Rebecca___

Hurrah! about your
Presentation
Your Poster was colorful
and detailed.
Hurrah!
Your voice was
clear and interesting.

Hint... Next time, you could
use a pointer to show what
Part you're talking about.

From ___Anne___

Figure 14.
2 stars and a wish
(Reproducible master
in appendix)

To ___Ben___   From ___Sally___
about your painting
Two Stars

☆ Great colors!

☆ You filled in the whole space.

A Wish

Wish
You'd sign your work so
we'd know who the
artist is.

Activity: Quality Control

Why

To help students learn to self-assess so they can produce the best quality of whatever they are doing

How

- Talk with students about what quality is in different areas. We use specific examples like, "What does a good reader sound like?" "What makes a high-quality piece of writing?" "What makes a musical performance memorable?" Guide your students to discuss substance as well as surface features.

- Choose an example that applies to the work your class is doing and have students suggest what describes a quality piece of work or performance. List the responses and display them in the classroom so students can refer to them.

- Provide time and reminders during class for students to check for "quality control."

- Encourage them to get feedback from other students.

Learning Link: How can I adapt this activity?

_____

_____

Activity: Criteria Count

Why

To establish expectations for work or performance

How

- Talk with students about the importance of knowing what counts or what is expected for a task or performance.

- Choose a relevant example for your class and start by asking students, "What makes a good _____?" Try doing "literacy commercials" in your classrooms: have students stand and "sell" a book they have read. (We have used setting criteria for commercials in the example below (see figure 15)).

Figure 15.
Criteria count
for book
commercials

> **CRITERIA COUNT FOR BOOK COMMERCIALS:**
> 1. Enthusiasm for the book and the audience.
> 2. Use a clear voice that everyone can hear.
> 3. Sell the book so that others want to read it.
> 4. Be creative!

Note: Once you start developing criteria with your students, they will use criteria for everything! Colleen's students even have criteria for cleaning up the classroom. If you feel you would like more information on criteria, an excellent reference is *Setting and Using Criteria* (Gregory, Cameron, and Davies 1997).

- Ask students, "What makes a good commercial?" List their responses on large strips of paper that can be moved. Use the students' ideas, but if they have left out a critical point, contribute it. Sort the responses into three to five main ideas and label each category. Display the criteria so students can refer to them.

- Review the criteria before students do their commercials. When students have presented their commercials, ask them to self-check the criteria to see how they did. (When we have set criteria for a specific task and students have worked through the process a few times, we prepare a Criteria Count sheet, which they can use before, during, and after their assignment.)

Learning Link: How can I adapt this activity?

_____

_____

Activity: Specific Compliments

Why

To give students feedback that has specific information

How

- Talk with students about general and specific compliments. A general compliment is one that may make us feel good. A specific compliment makes us feel recognized, gives us definite information, and makes us feel good because someone has focused on a special quality of our work or performance.

- Choose three students who are willing and able to demonstrate a skill like reading, singing, dancing, or karate. Ask students to give specific compliments, then ask the performer, "What specific information did the compliment give you?" If a student gives a general compliment like, "You did a good job," agree and ask, "What did you notice that would make you say that?" Work with students to get them to put content into their compliments.

■ Modeling is critical if you want students to develop the ability to give specific compliments. Every time you hear a student say, "It was good," add, "I agree. What about it made you think it was good?" (If adults come to visit our young students and give them a general compliment, the students often ask, "What exactly did you like about it?")

Learning Link: How can I adapt this activity?

_____

_____

Activity: Reflection

> *"To read without reflecting is like eating without digesting."*
> **—Edmund Burke,** in *The Teacher's Quotation Book*

Why

To give students an ongoing way to appreciate and improve their learning

How

■ Talk with students about the value of taking time to look at and think about what they have done so they can appreciate their efforts and think about what they will do next time.

■ Ask students three questions after they complete an assignment, an activity, or a project: "What do you like about it, what would you change, and what would you do another time?" The few minutes it takes to stop and reflect have an incredible payoff in the quality of work students do.

■ Reflection can take several forms: self-talk, personal writing, partner or small-group discussion, or a whole-class meeting. The first three are about students' personal efforts and the last is a way to check the feelings of the group. Once or twice a week, schedule time to meet as a whole group and ask, "How did we do on cleanup today?" or "What kinds of things did we do to help each other this week?"

■ Give the students a frame like 2 Hurrahs and a Hint (see appendix).

Learning Link: How can I adapt this activity?

_____

_____

Activity: Subject Snapshot

Why

To capture and display growth over time in a subject area

How

- Talk with students about ways their family pictures or "snapshots" show how they have grown and changed over time.

- Tell students they can do the same thing with "snapshots" of their progress in a subject area.

- Decide how many times and when you want to collect samples. (We collect snapshots three or four times a year to accompany reports. Many teachers of young students collect beginning-of-school year and end-of-school year samples; some teachers collect samples each month.)

- Give students a folded piece of tag board or two file folders taped together so they have a way to hold and display their work samples.

Note: For examples of forms for reflection, see _Together Is Better_ (Davies et al. 1992). For more information on organizing students' collections of work, see the section on progress folios in _Multi-Age and More_ (Politano and Davies 1994) and _Recognition Without Rewards_ (Cameron et al. 1997).

- Pick a specific subject area and early in the school year or term have students do a dated, representative sample of their work and fasten it to their folder. Repeat the process according to the schedule you have decided on.

- Use samples as a way for students to notice how their work has changed and to set goals.

- Some teachers encourage students to do a written reflection to accompany each sample.

Learning Link: How can I adapt this activity?

_____

_____

Emotions Activities

*To do well in our lives means we first must understand
what it means to use emotion intelligently.*

— Daniel Goleman, *Emotional Intelligence*

Activity: Snowball Fight

Why

To give students a way to vent negative feelings about a topic and
to clear the air

How

- Talk with students about the need to deal with negative feelings.

- Tell students that some topics or situations have negative as well
  as positive feelings attached to them and that good learning
  cannot happen unless those bad feelings are dealt with.

- Give students sheets of recycled paper and ask them to write
  words or phrases that describe their negative feelings.

- Once they have written several words, have students scrunch up
  the paper into a "snowball."

- On a given signal, have the students throw their snowballs,
  retrieve others, and throw them again.

- After students have had a chance to throw the snowballs several
  times, collect the snowballs and put them in the recycle bin.

- Have students meet with a partner to talk about what they wrote
  and why.

- Encourage students to give each other suggestions and support on
  how to deal with the negative feelings.

Learning Link: How can I adapt this activity?

_____

_____

Activity: Compliment Chain

Why

To build positive feelings and classroom community

How

■ Talk with students about the importance of being recognized.

■ Choose one student to be recognized (V.I.P., birthday, student of the day, classroom council, someone who needs a boost—every student will have a turn by the end of the year).

■ Give the other students a 22 cm x 5 cm (8 1/2" x 2") strip of paper.

■ Ask each student to write one positive comment about the person being recognized.

■ When they finish writing on the strip of paper, have students take the paper to the person being recognized. That person then reads the comments silently and makes a paper chain out of the strips. (Our young students like to make necklaces out of them; older students may not wear them, but they treasure them just the same.)

Learning Link: How can I adapt this activity?

_____

_____

Activity: Me, Too!

Why

To establish relationships by helping students find common interests or experiences

How

■ Talk with students about the value of making connections through shared interests.

- Tell students that they are going to do an activity that requires them to get up and move around when they hear a comment that applies to them.

- Explain that you are going to talk about something that several students may have done (for example, gone swimming, read a good book, seen a new movie). As soon as you are through speaking, ask all students who have done what you described to put up their hand and move to another student whose hand is up.

- When they find a partner, the students have fifteen seconds to share their experience.

- To start the activity, be sure to use prompts that most students can relate to (for example, if you got out of bed more than an hour ago, half an hour ago, ten minutes ago; if you walked to school, rode in a car, came in a bus, rode a bike).

Learning Link: How can I adapt this activity?

Activity: Expert Name Tags

Why

To help students recognize and acknowledge their own expertise

How

- Talk with students about the value of acknowledging their own expertise.

- Tell students that each of them is an expert in some way (for example, Lego builder, computer whiz, editor, artist), but unless they know one another well, they will not know who has skills that can be helpful.

- Give the students name badges (large enough to write their name and some comments on).

- Ask each student to write his or her name on the tag, large enough so that it can be easily seen.

- Have students think of some skills or qualities they have, and write or draw these on their name tag.

- Have students walk around to greet one another and read one another's name tags.

■ Bring the group together and invite students to tell what they discovered about one another.

Learning Link: How can I adapt this activity?

_____

_____

Activity: Shelving It!

Why

To help students temporarily put aside problems, worries, and issues that could keep them from focusing

How

■ Talk with students about what happens in our brain (and with our emotions) when we have something that preoccupies our thinking.

■ Tell students that sometimes we have concerns so overwhelming that we cannot put them aside. For less pressing issues, however, we can learn ways to put our concerns on hold so that we can get on with classroom learning.

■ Have students write the problem down. That way, they will know that you are not asking them to dismiss their worry. Rather, you are asking them to set it aside for now and take care of it later.

■ Once students have written down the problem, have them put it on a "problem shelf" or in a "worry box."

Learning Link: How can I adapt this activity?

_____

_____

Activity: Personal Success Stories

Why

To give students an opportunity to share their stories of personal wisdom, to feel good about themselves, and to provide other students with role models, support, and examples of problem solving

How

- Talk with students about how, by sharing their strategies for success, they can help one another.

- When a student has a dilemma, ask other students if they have ever found a successful way to deal with a similar situation.

- To avoid "tabloid-style" stories and embarrassment for the student, ask students to make a quick outline, or some notes about their solution.

- After you have had a chance to look through the success stories, ask individuals to mentor and listen to the person who was having the problem.

- At a later time, check with the students to see if the success stories helped.

Learning Link: How can I adapt this activity?

_____

_____

Activity: The Storm

Why

To provide a soothing transition when students enter the classroom

How

- Talk with students about why you are doing this activity—explain that it is one that is calming and will help to get them into a positive learning state.

- Have students sit in a large circle.

- Without talking, have one student (or you) start the action. The actions are:

  - snapping fingers

  - tapping thighs lightly

  - tapping thighs harder

  - kicking feet up and down

  - kicking feet stops

- tapping thighs hard

- tapping thighs lightly

- snapping fingers

- resting hands

- Have the first action move clockwise from one person to the next.

- When the first action has gone around the circle and everyone is doing it, have the leader stop that action and start the next one, and so on.

Learning Link: How can I adapt this activity?

_____

_____

CHAPTER EIGHT
Meaning Activities

Meaning is enveloped in the ideas that live on in our lives.
— Caine, Caine, and Crowell, *MindShifts*

Activity: Browse, Borrow, and Build

Why

To let students look at what others are doing and then to validate and add to their own thinking

How

- Talk with students about the value of looking at others' work and using information from those works in their own.

- Have students choose a variety of methods to represent (see pages 38–39) or show what they know about a topic (students can use any representational form; for example, drawing, building, or writing).

- When students have had sufficient time to complete a first draft, have them walk around and look at what other students are doing (browsing).

- Encourage students to collect ideas they could add or incorporate into their own work (borrowing).

- Have students return to their own work and adapt or include ideas they have gathered (building).

Learning Link: How can I adapt this activity?

Note: You can use this idea more than once during an ongoing project.

Why

To get students to make meaning by talking through an idea and listening to others (this encourages students to go beyond their friendship group)

How

- Talk with students about the learning possibilities when they talk with other learners.

- Provide students with appointment books A, B, and C (see appendix) for recording their appointments. (Some of the ones we have liked best are: a page out of an appointment book, a clock face, a theme-related form such as the four seasons, four lobes, five senses, or eight intelligences.)

- Explain that each person will need to move around the group and set up appointments. For example, "Do you have any openings? Will you be my two o'clock appointment?" Have students fill in

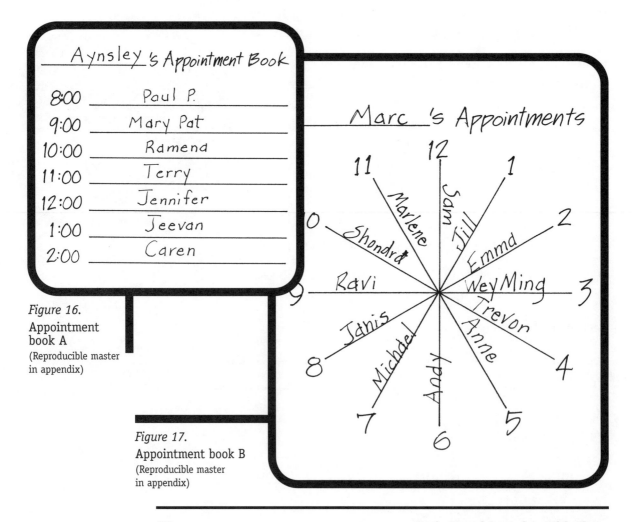

Figure 16.
Appointment
book A
(Reproducible master
in appendix)

Figure 17.
Appointment book B
(Reproducible master
in appendix)

their appointment book by writing someone's name beside the specified time; their name goes into the other person's form at the same time.

■ Give students two minutes to meet with other students to fill out their appointment schedule.

■ Have students who have empty spaces in their appointment times come to a designated area in the room to find classmates to meet with.

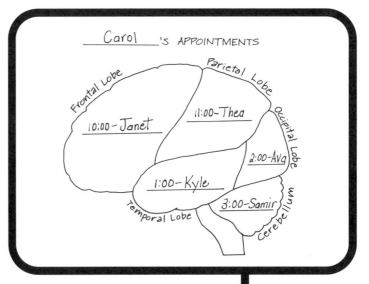

Figure 18.
Appointment book C
(Reproducible master in appendix)

■ When you need your students to talk to each other, say something like, "Meet with your eleven o'clock appointment to review the four lobes of the brain."

Learning Link: How can I adapt this activity?

_____

_____

Activity: Themes and Concepts

Why

To give students a common focus, which allows them to pursue aspects of a topic that are relevant and meaningful to them. Through themes we can integrate curricular strands. A student who is strong in math, for example, develops understanding in that area and then applies his or her insights to other disciplines.

> *People learn by making connections, and our ability to connect is enhanced when we see the larger context for what is being learned.*
>
> **—Anne Davies et al.,** *Making Themes Work*

How

■ Talk with students and brainstorm their ideas for major topics of study.

■ Show students the provincial or state overview of curriculum or requirements and match this list to students' suggestions.

Establish which student choices correlate with the mandated curriculum, then involve students in a discussion of how to fit the "leftovers" into theme or concept studies.

■ Take a large calendar or time line to establish theme topics and time frames. This is simply a guide that can easily be adjusted depending on students' needs and interests. Allow time for those "teachable moments," which sometimes turn into mini-themes.

> *For those students who like routine and structure, this "We are here and this is where we're going," overview provides a sense of the big picture. It also serves as a way to show how one topic or theme can be connected to many others—another opportunity to make meaning.*

■ Post your theme overview for easy viewing and access so you can refer to it, alter it, and add strategies and processes you have used and connections you have made.

■ Start each theme or topic with WIIFM and SWYAK and end with a celebration. Go back to the calendar/time line and record three or four of the most significant memories of the theme studied.

Learning Link: How can I adapt this activity?

_____

_____

Activity: Yours, Mine, and Ours

Why

To provide students with a structure for expressing their own ideas, listening to others' ideas, and then developing a list of common concepts

How

■ Talk with students about their uniqueness and the importance of hearing one another's knowledge, ideas, and opinions to help gather new information. Explain they will be working through a process to record and share their own ideas, construct some commonalities, and share them with the large group. Tell them that within each group they will need a recorder and a reporter.

■ Instruct students to use the form to record their own views in an established time limit (use form A for two students, form B for 3 students, or form C for 4 students (see appendix)).

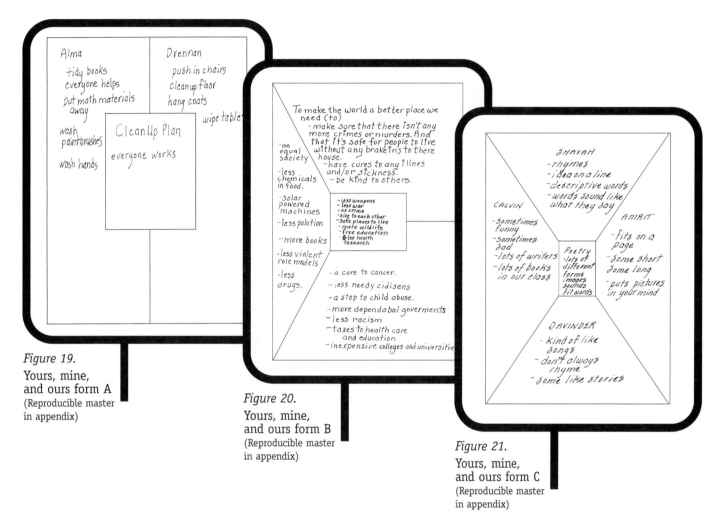

Figure 19.
Yours, mine, and ours form A
(Reproducible master in appendix)

Figure 20.
Yours, mine, and ours form B
(Reproducible master in appendix)

Figure 21.
Yours, mine, and ours form C
(Reproducible master in appendix)

■ Have each student read what he or she has written to the others.

■ Have students choose a recorder and a reporter for their group (or use established classroom routines for determining roles in cooperative groups).

■ Encourage the recorder to ask the members of the group which ideas everyone had in common, then record the ideas in the central section of the paper. Suggest each group try for four common statements. Check in during the process, asking, "How many groups have at least two or more ideas?" (We experienced Eric Jensen using this check-in technique and appreciated the way it helped our groups feel successful.)

- Once students have recorded their common ideas, ask them to priorize their list.

- Gather students together and have the reporter for each group read the group's first two statements.

Learning Link: How can I adapt this activity?

_____

_____

Activity: Storytelling

Why

To help students make meaning on two levels: (1) the meaning of the words they are listening to, and (2) the personal meaning they make relating the story to their own experiences. We know that learning facts in isolation is difficult because there is no connective thread; setting those facts in a narrative form puts them in context.

How

- Talk with students about the ways stories help us make meaning.

- Demonstrate to students the value of creating, reading, and listening to stories as a vehicle for learning: Give students a list of ten words, time to study the list, and then ask them to write the words from memory. Give students another list of ten words, tell them a story that includes those words, give them time to study the list, retell the story, and ask them to write the list of words from memory. Have them talk about which list of words was easier to remember and why.

- As you work your way through a theme, look for and ask students to find related stories.

- Teach your students the basics of learning and remembering a story. Here are some of Joy's tips:

  - Find a story that jumps off the pages—you cannot tell a story that you do not like!

  - Read the story several times, taking notes of key words or phrases.

  - Never, ever try to memorize the story.

  - For visual learners, draw the story and use that as a script.

- For auditory learners, record yourself telling the story and view or listen to it.

- For kinesthetic learners, make or find some props, or use Knots on a Rope (see page 101).

- Practice telling the story a few times (family pets are a great audience!).

- Never apologize if you have forgotten part of the story. Instead, say something like, "Did I tell...." or "Don't forget this..."

Note: This activity works as well with older students in a variety of content areas.

Colleen says, "When you read poetry to kids, they start writing poems." Joy has found the same thing happens when she tells stories in her classroom—the kids become storytellers, too.

Learning Link: How can I adapt this activity?

_____

_____

Activity: Each One, Teach One

Why

To demonstrate mastery of a topic by teaching it to other students. Before we teach something to someone else, we need to know it and understand it well ourselves.

How

- Talk with students about the value of teaching others—to teach something, you need to know and understand it well. For this activity, each student can teach someone else something about a common topic, or each student can take responsibility for preparing and presenting to a small group or the whole group.

- Ask students about possible audiences: buddy classes, younger students in the school, parents and grandparents, day-care friends, or other students in the classroom.

- Choose a time, during or at the end of a theme or unit of study, when students have had an opportunity to master the content or a process.

- Provide a sheet or schedule for presenters or sessions so that interested students can sign up.

- After students have taught their material, ask them to reflect on what went well and what they would do another time. Tell the students being taught to give some feedback to their teacher. One of our favorite formats is 2 Stars and a Wish (see appendix).

Learning Link: How can I adapt this activity?

_____

_____

Activity: Fire the Neurons!

Why

To help students be more successful by accessing prior knowledge and tapping into established connections

How

- Talk with students about how neurons work together as networks, explaining that when we are learning something new it is important to connect with what we already know. Once we have one association, this helps us "fire up" other connections and gain access to a network of ideas.

- Before starting an activity, give students time to make some personal connections, literacy connections, mathematical connections, and experiential connections (SWYAK, writing, drawing, talking, reading related material, watching a video, looking at photographs).

- With our young students, we encourage them to begin a new book by talking about what is on the cover. We suggest they talk about the title and the pictures, and predict what words they might see and what the book might be about. We encourage students to use the pattern, "The connections I'm making are...," or to speculate what kind of neural firing is going on in their brain.

- Meet with students to discuss how the "firing" helped them make meaning.

Learning Link: How can I adapt this activity?

_____

_____

Multi-Path Activities

Speaking, writing, computing, drawing, art, playing music, singing, moving gracefully in dancing and sports: the development of our knowledge goes hand in hand with the development of the skills that support that knowledge.

— Carla Hannaford, *Smart Moves*

Activity: VAK (Visual, Auditory, and Kinesthetic)

Why

To help students and teachers use and understand learning senses; to discover personal strengths and preferences when perceiving, processing, and presenting information

How

■ Talk with the students about VAK learning senses, introducing the terms *visual, auditory*, and *kinesthetic*. In the discussion, ask students to give their ideas of what each term means. Explain to students that most learners have some strengths in each learning sense, but often we are stronger in one or two of the senses.

■ Display the overhead transparency of figure 22 (see appendix) that lists the characteristics of visual, auditory, and kinesthetic learners. Give students a copy or a piece of paper; have them fold it in thirds and mark one section "visual," one section "auditory," and one section "kinesthetic."

■ Read the characteristics of a visual learner together. Tell students to put a check for each statement that describes them. Repeat for auditory and kinesthetic categories.

■ Ask students to add the number of checks they have in each category.

■ Tell students if they have four or more checks in a category, that shows they are probably strong in this learning sense. Some people are very strong in one sense, while others may have equal strengths in each of the senses.

Note: We have found VAK to be a useful tool for planning because it helps us balance our program for all learners (not just our own preferred senses). VAK has also been a useful tool for our students when they present their learning using visual, auditory, and kinesthetic representations.

Learning Senses

Visual Learner

- learns best from visual information
- observes details around him or her
- usually does not find noise distracting
- finds it easier to remember what he or she sees
- likes to make eye contact
- speaks quickly
- makes mental pictures
- tends to remember what he or she sees rather than what he or she hears
- is often a good speller
- prefers to read rather than give a speech
- enjoys writing
- likes to look at artwork
- tends to doodle
- prefers to give a demonstration rather than give a speech
- may forget to pass on a verbal message
- needs the big purpose and a sense of purpose
- needs instructions and materials to be written as well as given verbally

Auditory Learner

- learns best from verbal information
- talks to himself/herself
- usually finds noise distracting
- finds it easier to remember what he or she hears
- tends to be talkative; relishes discussions
- speaks rhythmically with tone, pitch, and volume
- is able to mimic speech patterns and sounds
- tends to be an eloquent speaker
- often reviews conversations mentally
- is more able to spell orally than in writing
- likes to read aloud and listen
- enjoys listening to music
- prefers to express his or her ideas orally
- likes jokes better than comics
- prefers to tell information rather than write it down

Kinesthetic Learner

- learns best from physical input
- likes to move and be active
- finds it easier to remember what he or she does physically
- often touches others to get their attention
- speaks slowly
- memorizes by walking and doing
- large muscles develop early
- tracks print with finger when he or she is reading
- does better by doing a task rather than by reading or hearing about it
- handwriting may be messy
- likes games and drama
- uses action words
- uses gestures to communicate
- finds it difficult to sit still
- needs action
- prefers to use the body to show what he or she knows
- likes to be comfortable

Figure 22.
Characteristics of visual, auditory, and kinesthetic learners
(Reproducible master in appendix)

- Talk with students about how knowing about their learning senses can be helpful. Record ideas on a chart and post the chart for reference.

- After you have talked about VAK, teach a specific strategy for each of the learning senses. When students are comfortable using all three senses, they sometimes have a choice of using the one that suits them best. Occasionally, you might want to challenge them by asking them to use a different learning sense.

- When students understand VAK learning senses, they have a tool for making meaning and expressing their understanding. If students are reading something that does not make sense to them, encourage them to try a VAK tool. The visual strategy would be to draw or sketch the main ideas; the auditory strategy would be to talk about what they have read or have someone read the material to them and then talk about it; the kinesthetic strategy would be to make a model or do an activity like Knots on a Rope (see page 101).

Learning Link: How can I adapt this activity?

_____

_____

Activity: Representing

Why

To give students opportunities to show what they know in ways that best suit their personal learning styles

How

- Talk with students about uniqueness and how just as our backgrounds, experiences, and ways of thinking vary, we show our understanding in different ways. The process of representing helps us clarify our thinking.

- Ask students to brainstorm different ways that people show what they know. Ask which of those ways are possible to do within the classroom because of limited space and time, and availability and expense of materials. As the students contribute suggestions, put the suggestions on strips of paper that can be sorted and categorized. (These strips can be reused with students when planning ways to represent various tasks.) You may establish different lists with your students. The lists below are suggestions for possibilities for representation. The materials required for most of the suggestions are usually available in classrooms. You can expand the range of representation depending on your resources, budget, and available time.

Verbal: advertisement, audio-tape, audiobiography, character sketch, debate, interview, job description, limerick, list, news broadcast, monologue, oral report, panel discussion, poetry reading or recitation, question period, radio show, rap, riddles, song, storytelling, talk show, weather report

Action: card game, commercial, construction, cooking, court-trial, dance, demonstration, exhibition, experiment, game show, mime, model, musical presentation, play, puppet show, rap, role drama, skit, video

Paper with pencil, pens, crayons: activity book, acrostics, advertisement, advice column, autobiography, banner, bibliography, booklet, brochure, cartoon, chart, collage, comic strip, cookbook, crossword puzzle, diagram, diary, dictionary, drawing, editorial, essay, fairy tale, flip book, flow chart, game board, graph, illustration, job description, letter, limerick, list, magazine article, map, mural, news-paper article, pamphlet, paragraph, poem, poster, puzzle, report, research paper, reviews, riddles, sequence chart, scrolls, sociogram, storyboard, time line. If the budget allows, these activities can be done on the computer, with a camera, or with special art materials like paints, pastels, chalk, inks, drawing pencils, charcoal.

Three dimensional: collection, display, diorama, game, mobile, model, papier-mâché, project cube, sculpture

- After completing your classroom list of ways to represent, choose a topic and give your students time to plan, make, and share their representations. It is important to allow students to use the same form of representation several times so they can develop and refine techniques. At the same time, encourage students to try different ways so they build "a repertoire of representing."

- To keep a record of representations, have students use various formats, such as lists, learning logs, bingo cards, graphs, webs, and photograph albums.

Learning Link: How can I adapt this activity?

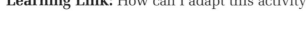

_____

_____

Activity: Museum Walkabout

Why

To give students an opportunity to view and discuss one another's work

How

- Talk with students about the value of looking at other's work and about having someone to share ideas with. Talk about "museum etiquette"—talking quietly, moving appropriately, and not touching things.

  - Tell students that when they are perusing one another's projects, they should act in the same manner and show the same respect that they would if they were walking around in a museum looking at masterpieces or exhibits.

    - Tell students they can go to the museum by themselves, but it is more beneficial to have someone to share their responses with.

    - Have students find a partner and begin the "walkabout" around the classroom.

  - Have students come together as a group to discuss what impressed them and any ideas they might want to incorporate into their work.

Learning Link: How can I adapt this activity?

_____

_____

Activity: Presenting

Why

To give students an audience for sharing their representations

How

- Talk with students about the benefits of sharing representations. It is beneficial to talk about what you did, your product, and how you did it—your process.

- Remember, there are alternatives to having the whole group witness each student's presentation at one sitting (see Staggered Show and Tell, page 114; 4-Corner Presentations, page 57; and Museum Walkabout; page 86).

  - Provide students with time to rehearse, then choose an organizational system for scheduling presentations.

    - Some teachers capture students on videotape to record the different kinds of representations and their growth and development in presenting.

    - Establish ways for students to give constructive feedback in response to presentations (for example: 2 Hurrahs and a Hint, see page 64; Compliment Chain, see page 70; Yours, Mine, and Ours, see page 78; Criteria Count, see page 65; Quality Control, see page 65; and 2 Stars and a Wish, see page 64).

- Set the tone for celebration by using music, cheers, ovations, and waves.

Learning Link: How can I adapt this activity?

_____

_____

Note: We know there are benefits in getting feedback. Viewing other representations helps trigger ideas; seeing peers' models helps us conceive possibilities for ourselves. Sharing representations is a critical part of creating a brain-based environment. It gives us a way to recognize and celebrate the uniqueness of each learner. Even though it is tempting to gloss over or skip sharing because of time pressures, it is important that you find ways to build sharing time into your class schedule: you will see such positive results with your students.

Activity: Multiple Intelligence Time (M.I.T.)

Why

To help students understand and expand the ways they think and represent

How

- Talk with students about Howard Gardner's theory of intelligences, specifically, the eight intelligences: linguistic, logical-mathematical, spatial, musical, bodily-kinesthetic, interpersonal, intrapersonal, and naturalistic. With young students, use the following terms to tell them about different ways to be smart:

  - linguistic: word smart

  - logical-mathematical: math smart

- spatial: art smart

- musical: music smart

- bodily-kinesthetic: game smart

- interpersonal: people smart

- intrapersonal: self smart

- naturalistic: nature smart

- Ask students to think of people who fit into each of the categories (including local celebrities or particularly talented classroom members). These are the choices our students made this year:

  - word smart: Robert Munsch

  - math smart: Count from *Sesame Street*

  - art smart: Georgia O'Keefe

  - music smart: Mozart

  - game smart: Michael Jordan

  - people smart: Mother Teresa

  - self smart: Will Rogers

  - nature smart: Johnny Appleseed

- You can use this list in two ways: (1) as a reminder of what it means to be, for example, "word smart" or "people smart," or (2) as titles for centers that have been set up with appropriate materials for each of the intelligences.

- If you set up MI centers, you might want to include the following materials:

  - word smart: paper, pens, dictionaries, computer

  - math smart: calculators, abacus, dice, playing cards, manipulatives, blocks, geometric s-shapes and solids

  - art smart: paper, paints, pastels, crayons, pencils, chalk, colored pens, scissors, glue, 3-D materials, sewing supplies

  - music smart: tape recorder or CD player, listening center with headphones, tapes or CDs, musical instruments (not drums!), sheet music

  - game smart: board games, jacks, skipping ropes, marbles, blocks, "nerf" balls, beanbags

  - people smart: puppet theater, costumes, drama props, cooperative games

- self-smart: personal journals, novels, biographies, nonfiction books, magazines

- nature smart: nonfiction books, nature collections, classroom pet, things to sort and classify

■ Give the students several days to experience working and learning at each of the MI centers.

■ When students complete M.I.T. (multiple intelligence time) each day, meet as a whole group and ask students to talk about where they worked, the processes they used, and any products they have made.

Learning Link: How can I adapt this activity?

_____

_____

Activity: Multiple Intelligence Graphs

Why

To record and reflect on ways of thinking and representing

How

■ Talk with students about their capabilities in each of the eight intelligences. Remind them that most people have strengths and preferences in how they think and do things.

■ Talk with students about the centers they have been working at during M.I.T. Ask:

- Did you find yourself going back to the same centers?

- Which centers did you visit most often?

- Which center did you like best?

- Which center were you the most successful at?

- Is there a center you did not go to?

- Did you try a new center after you saw what someone else was doing or making at it?

■ Explain to students they will have several more opportunities to work at the M.I.T. centers. At the end of each working session, they will be given a graph to record where they have worked that day.

- Give students a copy of the M.I. graph of learning (see appendix) and with an overhead transparency explain to them how they will use the graph to record which intelligences they have used. Explain to the students that even when they seem to be working in one intelligence, they are often using some skills that apply from another. For example, if they were working on writing and publishing a story, they would probably color the graph space under "word smart" to the maximum level. As well, they would have measured paper for a "book"cover for the story— using "math smart," even if it was for a small job. Therefore, they would color the graph space under "math smart" to the minimal level.

- After students have filled in five or six graphs, ask them to count the number of spaces they colored in each intelligence. Transfer that information onto a master graph and make some observations. Have students talk and write about what intelligences they feel strongest in and what intelligences they feel they would like to develop more.

- As you do different activities during the year, give students time to stop and assess which intelligences they are using, and to reflect on their growth and development.

Learning Link: How can I adapt this activity?

_____

_____

Figure 23.

M.I. graph of learning
(Reproducible master in appendix)

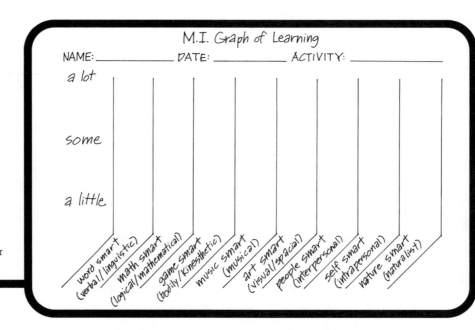

Activity: Charades

Why

To give students a novel, challenging way to present or review content without using language skills. This activity gives strong kinesthetic learners a chance to perform and visual and auditory learners an opportunity to build their skills.

How

- Talk with students about different ways to present information—most often information is presented verbally or visually. Explain to students that they are going to communicate using something other than verbal or visual cues.

- Tell students they are going to play charades. Charades is an effective, popular, and novel way to review content (for example, names of provinces and states; characters in literature, science, or history; titles of books).

- Explain the procedure for playing charades (everyone has their own version, so you need to come to agreement as a class). Joy uses these rules (your students will develop their own "signals" as they have more experience with playing charades):

  - A student acts out his or her charade without using any oral communication.

  - To start, the player uses his or her fingers to indicate how many words are in the charade.

  - To work on one word at a time, the player holds up a finger(s) to indicate which word is being worked on.

  - The player puts one finger or more on his or her forearm to indicate syllabication.

  - Three fingers up (in a "w" shape) stands for "who, where, when, why, what."

- To begin, have a list of charade words prepared for students to act out. With experience, students will generate their own lists.

Learning Link: How can I adapt this activity?

Brain-Body Activities

*The human qualities we associate with the mind
can never exist separate from the body.*

— Carla Hannaford, *Smart Moves*

Activity: Crossovers

Why

To give students a physical break that energizes their brains

How

■ Talk with students about the effects of taking a break—
particularly doing a physical activity that requires them to
"crossover." Remind students that during the day the two sides of
their brain take turns being in charge. Tell students you want to
help them use both sides of their brain because when they use
both hemispheres, they can do their best learning. Cross-lateral
activities activate the brain and force the two sides to talk to
each other.

■ Some standard "crossovers" are:

   ■ one hand to opposite side of back

   ■ hands to opposite knees, hips, elbows, heels, toes

   ■ roller coaster loops in front of face, with
one thumb, then the other

   ■ touch nose and hold opposite ear,
switch

■ Lead students through the first "crossovers" and
then leave them to do some on their own. In
time, you will find your kids will stand up during
the day and do "crossovers" whenever they feel
sluggish or need an instant energizer.

Learning Link: How can I adapt this activity?

_____

_____

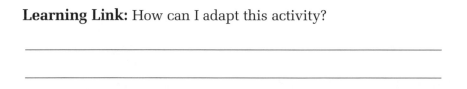

Activity: Ball Toss

Why

To include novelty and help students be alert and focused

How

■ Talk with students about interesting ways of taking turns during a lesson or an activity.

■ Use a sponge ball, a "Koosh" ball, or—our favorite—a sponge football in the shape of a brain.

■ Explain to the students that you will toss the ball. Whoever catches it is the first speaker. After that student has had his or her turn, he or she then tosses the ball to someone else.

■ If you are working in groups, have the designated speaker for each group stand and wait for the ball to be tossed to him or her.

■ As always, students have a choice to take their turn or pass the ball to someone else.

Learning Link: How can I adapt this activity?

_____

_____

Activity: Massage Circle

Why

To give students a relaxing, energizing break

How

■ Talk with students about the value of a relaxing break.

■ Have students stand in a circle, one behind the other.

■ Have students place their hands on the shoulders of the person in front of them and give that person a "light" massage (stress the word _light_).

- Make students responsible for telling their masseuse how the pressure is feeling.

- Tell students to thank their masseuse, then turn around the other way in the circle and start again.

Learning Link: How can I adapt this activity?

_____

_____

Activity: Human Links of Learning

Why

To give students a novel way of reviewing material learned during a lesson, theme, or unit of study

How

- Talk with students about the importance of review. Explain that review helps transfer learning to long-term memory. Also discuss the value of "linking" one piece of information to another.

- Tell students they are going to make a human chain. Ask one student to stand up and start the chain by making a statement about the topic you have been focusing on. As soon as that student has made his or her statement, another student stands up, links an arm with the first student, and says, "I can link to that..." (For example, if you were studying plants, the first student would stand up and might say, "Plants grow in the soil." The second student stands, links an arm through the first student's arm and says, "I can link to that. The soil gives the plant food." A third student stands, links an arm through the second student's arm and says, "I can link to that. The soil anchors the roots of the plant.") Have students add to the chain until they can no longer think of anything to add.

- Count how many links the students have made, then celebrate!

Learning Link: How can I adapt this activity?

_____

_____

Activity: Meaningful Mingling

Why

To mix movement and memory

How

- Talk with the students about the value of practicing different ways of learning and about the positive effect of movement and fun on learning.

  - Gather the students in a tight space.

    - Tell the students that when they hear the words, "Mingle, mingle, mingle," they are to shuffle around in a confined area until they hear (for example), "Stop. Tell the person closest to your right elbow three things you know about the brain." "Mingle, mingle, mingle." "Stop. Tell the person closest to your left ear something you did today that is good for your brain."

    - The mingling part of this activity is always the same and it is really fun. The talking part changes depending on the content of the lesson, theme, or unit of study the class is working on.

Learning Link: How can I adapt this activity?

_____

_____

Activity: Laugh Line

Why

To give students a novel, energizing break

How

- Talk with the students about the value of laughter. (Some responses we have heard are: "People enjoy laughing." "It's hard to feel anxious when you're laughing." "It's hard to feel threatened when you're happy.")

- Have the students form lines of five or six people.

- The first student starts to giggle, stops, and the second student starts a laugh, then the third student, and so on.

Brain-Based Learning With Class

- Soon the one-to-one chain of laughter becomes a wave of laughter and everyone is consumed with laughter.

Learning Link: How can I adapt this activity?

_____

_____

Activity: Role-Playing Review

Why

To help students remember material by having them assume the roles of expert and interviewer

How

- Talk with students about the value of role-playing as a way to review what they know.

- Talk to students about interviewing skills, then watch a video clip of an interview on a news broadcast, children's program, or science show.

- Identify and list four criteria for a good interview.

- Give students time to prepare interview questions and comments.

- Pair the students: one student will be the interviewer and the other student will be the expert.

- Give the students an allotted time frame for the interview. When the conversation is finished, remind the interviewer to thank the expert and give him or her some feedback.

- Have partners switch roles and repeat the process.

Learning Link: How can I adapt this activity?

_____

_____

Memory Activities

*It is the memory that enables a person to
gather roses in January.*

— Anonymous

Activity: Retelling—Finger Countdown

Why

To improve students' recall, comprehension, and vocabulary

How

- Talk with the students about their abilities to remember and the need for review and practice to facilitate the transfer of information from short-term to long-term memory.

- Demonstrate this strategy by reading or telling a story and showing students some specific techniques (for example, Visual Scripting, Auditory Ping-Pong, Knots on a Rope) for recall (see pages 100–102).

- Tell students one of the easiest ways to remember the most important features of a story or a lesson is to use their fingers to count off the main points. We call this Finger Countdown. This works because with only ten fingers you can focus on the main points and not get distracted by details.

- Read a story aloud, then ask students to give the main points of the story. As each main point is recalled, hold up a finger (start with your thumb for the first point, add your second finger for the next point, and so on) to mark each part of the story. If students give responses out of sequence, ask them to hold them until you reach that part of the story.

Note: Whenever students need to recall a sequence of events or series of points, they will find that Finger Countdown is such a quick and effective strategy that it becomes the first step in any retelling activity.

Learning Link: How can I adapt this activity?

_____

_____

Activity: Retelling—Visual Scripting

Note: Once students have learned retelling strategies, they will find them useful for helping them to remember any content across the curriculum (for example, social studies: time sequence; science: parts of a flower; math: process of division).

Why

To give students a visual tool for memory or comprehension; to recall a story, the main points of a science, social studies, or math lesson, or any other curricular focus

How

■ Talk with students about learning senses (VAK).

■ Tell students visual scripting works well for visual learners. Explain that actors use something called a "script," which tells them what to say. Tell the students they will be creating a script of their own, which will help them remember what to say. Their script can have both pictures and words.

■ To demonstrate this strategy, read or tell a story to the whole class.

■ Do a Finger Countdown (retelling strategy, page 99) with the class.

■ Group students in pairs or triads, give each group a large piece of paper (at least 28 cm x 43 cm; 11" x 17"), and tell them to create a script that helps them recall the main points of the story. Tell students they have a time limit of ten minutes, so they do not have time for detail, only main points. Also assure them that their scripts are for their eyes only, so the perfectionist in the group does not have to worry about the final product.

■ Call time and instruct students to take turns retelling each part of the story. Have them use their script as visual clues.

■ Your students will probably each want their own copy of their script; make them each a copy, which they can use for review or for retelling to their families.

Learning Link: How can I adapt this activity?

_____

_____

Activity: Retelling—Auditory Ping-Pong

Why

To give students an auditory tool for memory or comprehension; to recall a story, the main points of a science, social studies, or math lesson, or any other curricular focus

How

- Talk with students about learning senses (VAK).

- Tell students this strategy works well for auditory learners who recall by talking and listening to others. This strategy is like Ping-Pong because you go back and forth like a Ping-Pong ball; it is different because you will be in a partnership instead of opposing each other.

- To demonstrate this strategy, read or tell a story to the whole class.

- Do a Finger Countdown (retelling strategy, page 99) with the class.

- Group students in pairs and have them sit "eyes to eyes, knees to knees." One student is "A," the other "B." "A" starts by telling the first main part of the story, "B" tells the next thing, and back and forth until the story is complete.

Learning Link: How can I adapt this activity?

_____

_____

Activity: Retelling—Knots on a Rope

Why

To give students a kinesthetic tool for memory or comprehension; to recall a story, the main points of a science, social studies, or math lesson, or any other curricular focus

How

- Talk with students about learning senses (VAK).

- Tell them this strategy works well for kinesthetic learners.

- To demonstrate the strategy, read or tell a story to the whole class.

- Do a Finger Countdown (retelling strategy, page 99) with the class.

- Give each student a piece of cord about 60 cm (2 feet) long (Joy likes to use Phentex, available at craft and chain stores).

  - Ask students to retell the main parts of the story; for each main point have students put a knot in their rope.

    - When the main points have been noted (no, knotted!), group the students into pairs, triads, or foursomes and have each group find an area to sit down at. Have the students assign themselves a number or letter and take turns retelling the main parts of the story, using the knots on the rope as kinesthetic clues.

    - Give students a strip of paper or a tag to label the rope with the title of the lesson or story. Students can use the knots in the rope for reviewing the lesson or story in class, or they can take the rope home and share the lesson or story with family.

Learning Link: How can I adapt this activity?

_____

_____

Activity: Meaning and Memory Maps

Why

To give students a visual, graphic organizer that helps with their comprehension and recall

How

Note: We use Meaning and Memory Maps for students to show their prior knowledge, check understanding during a theme or unit of study, after field trips, guest speakers, demonstrations, and lessons.

- Talk with students about the value of showing their thinking so that they can reflect on it. Explain that maps and webs activate both sides of the brain because they incorporate a combination of pictures, symbols, words, color, and styles of print. Meaning and memory maps organize information in a way that makes sense to learners.

- Demonstrate a map, using a topic that everyone knows. Write the title of the map on a blank page and enclose it in a shape. Organize and label main ideas in categories, branching out from the title. Personalize your map by adding relevant details with different colored pens, pictures, and symbols and different styles of print to highlight key points.

- Have students make a meaning and memory map of a recent classroom focus (see figure 24).

- Have students pause during their map making, stand up, and walk around to observe other maps (remind students of Browse, Borrow, and Build, page 75, and add to their own map).

- Give students time to talk with others about their maps.

- Give students opportunities to add to their maps throughout a theme or unit of study.

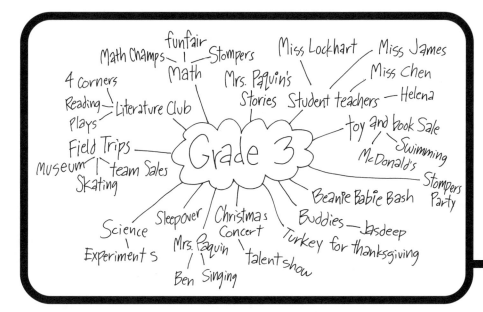

Figure 24. Meaning and memory map

Learning Link: How can I adapt this activity?

_____

_____

Activity: Brain Blueprints

Why

To give students another way of recalling information by associating what needs to be remembered with familiar locations

How

- Talk with students about how they can use something they know to help them remember something they are learning. Just as they have used a list of familiar "pegs" to help them remember things they needed to learn, they can use familiar locations to help them recall.

- Have students watch as you walk around the classroom noting significant features. Say things like, "I'm walking through the door, past the bookshelves, over to the windows, and around to the CD player."

- Walk back to the door and, this time as you follow the same path, make the associations, such as, "As I walk through the door, I think of walking into my forehead toward the frontal lobe. As I pass the bookshelves, I feel myself turning the pages of a book and I think of the parietal lobe. I walk to the windows and see the occipital lobe. When I walk to the CD player, I hear the music in my temporal lobe."

- Ask students to draw a map of their home or their bedroom and use the location to make personal associations to help them remember concepts they have been working on.

- Ask students to try this strategy at home, reflect on it, and tell how it worked for them. (We have noticed our kinesthetic learners are especially successful with this strategy.)

Learning Link: How can I adapt this activity?

_____

_____

Activity: Picture This

Why

To help students be more successful by giving them an opportunity to plan and organize before they do an activity

How

- Talk with students about the value of doing a mental "walk-through," and of making a picture plan before doing an activity.

- Choose an activity such as a field trip, an assembly, a science experiment, a group presentation, or cooking.

- Explain to the students the procedures they will be using for the selected activity.

- Give students large pieces of paper and have them work in cooperative groups to talk about and draw the steps they will follow when they are doing the activity (students may choose to add comments or labels).

- Meet with the large group to share picture plans.

- Encourage students to use their plan or review it while they do the activity.

- Meet with students following the completion of the activity to evaluate how the picture plans worked.

Learning Link: How can I adapt this activity?

_____

_____

Activity: Add-Ons

Why

To give students a novel and entertaining way to review and remember terms and names after a theme or unit of study

How

- Talk with students about ways they can adapt games to help them remember.

- Teach students to play Add-Ons. Start by having the first student say something like, "I'm going to brain school and I'm going to learn about one brain." The second student says, "I'm going to brain school and I'm going to learn about one brain and two hemispheres." The third student says, "I'm going to brain school and I'm going to learn about one brain, two hemispheres, and three systems for learning." Carry on as long as the students can keep going. If a student needs help, encourage other students to provide hints or clues.

- Another way to play this is to use alphabet letters. For instance, "I'm going on a picnic, and I want to take healthy food like apples." The second student says, "I'm going on a picnic and I want to take healthy food like apples and beets," and so on through the alphabet.

Learning Link: How can I adapt this activity?

_____

_____

CHAPTER TWELVE
Nutrition Activities

*A single tailor-made meal has the power to bring
about desired changes in concentration and
relaxation in as little as thirty minutes.*

— Joel Robertson and Tom Monte, *Peak-Performance Living*

Activity: Food Fact of the Week

Why

To give students information and engage them in discovering which
foods are good for learning and memory

How

- Talk with students about how some foods actually help
  learning and memory.

- Begin by discussing and posting a food fact of the week
  (see page 108).

- Each day, take four or five minutes to go over a food fact and
  invite students to talk about how they have applied the
  information to their own eating. (We have found that the more we
  talk about the value of certain foods, the more conscious our
  students become about trying to include the foods in their diets.
  Our young students, in fact, become quite zealous about what
  they need to eat.)

- Once several food facts have been presented, invite students to
  bring in facts they have discovered.

- Continue this activity throughout the year.

Learning Link: How can I adapt this activity?

Some Food Facts to Get You Started

- Eat protein to think better. Protein boosts alertness and mental performance. Protein contains tyrosine, a nutrient that manufactures dopamine, which raises awareness, and norepinephrine, which speeds thought transmission and boosts motivation. Foods high in protein include eggs, fish, tofu, pork, chicken, and yogurt. Most food guides recommend three servings of protein per day. The amount of protein you need depends on your age, size, and activity level; eating more than you need does not further increase alertness. Protein is the body's rocket fuel.

- Eat carbohydrates to relax. Carbohydrates contain tryptophan, which stimulates the production of the neurotransmitter serotonin. Serotonin helps you feel calm, less anxious, and sleep better. Serotonin relaxes the central nervous system, making you feel more confident. It gives you a feeling of well-being. Serotonin has been called the body's "peace train."

- Eat fruits and vegetables to boost learning. Fresh fruit and leafy green vegetables supply vitamins and minerals important for learning, memory, and intelligence. Folic acid found in leafy green vegetables reduces depression and boosts learning performance. Eating iron-rich foods like dark green vegetables improves attention, memory, perception, and visual motor-coordination.

- Eat calpain-rich foods. Calpain is a cleaner for the synapses. It dissolves protein build-up and makes the synapses more efficient for neural transmission. Calpain is found in dairy products—yogurt and milk are the best sources—and leafy green vegetables. Eat spinach and kale for more efficient thinking.

- Eat choline-rich foods to move better. Choline-rich foods are critical to the manufacture of the neurotransmitter acetylcholine. Acetylcholine takes its cues from the neurotransmitters around it and is associated with memory and smooth muscle movement. Soya beans and eggs are rich in choline.

- Drink water to be alert. Water is critical to brain function. The brain is composed of more than 70 percent water, a higher percentage of water than in any other organ. When you are dehydrated, you are less attentive and more lethargic. Eight glasses of water a day are essential to good thinking. The caffeine found in coffee, tea, and some soda drinks acts as a diuretic. Diuretics quickly remove water from the body, producing negative effects such as muscle tension and anxiety. If you wait until you are thirsty, you are already dehydrated. You need to drink water throughout the day.

Activity: Food Diary

Why

To help learners be aware of what they eat so they can use this information to make more brain-enhancing choices. (Some students have very little control over the quality or quantity of the food they eat. But, for those who do, information and self-awareness can help them make better choices.)

How

- Talk with students about what they know about nutrition and its role in optimal brain function. Bring in Canada's Food Guide or the American Nutrition Pyramid as a resource for your students.

This is a great opportunity to have a nutritionist as a guest speaker.

- Tell students that one way to become aware of what they eat is to record what they eat daily. Give students a copy of the food diary (see appendix) to record their daily food intake, their mood, and their energy and learning levels.

- At the end of one week, have students look at their food diaries with a partner. Encourage them to ask questions such as: "What food groups did I have enough of? What food groups do I need to work on getting more of? How did I feel? How was my learning level?" Ask students to set one positive eating goal for the next week.

- Have students do a second week of recording what they eat. Compare the results to the first week and discuss how well they did with their goal.

- Gather students together for a group discussion on which foods promoted good feelings, thinking, and learning.

Learning Link: How can I adapt this activity?

_____

_____

Food Diary

When you eat or drink - write it in your diary.
Fill in the circles so you can see that you are getting a balanced diet.

	Water	Protein	Milk products	Fruits	Vegetables	Grains
Monday	OOO OOO	OOO	OOO	OOO	OOO	OOO
Tuesday	OOO OOO	OOO	OOO	OOO	OOO	OOO
Wednesday	OOO OOO	OOO	OOO	OOO	OOO	OOO
Thursday	OOO OOO	OOO	OOO	OOO	OOO	OOO
Friday	OOO OOO	OOO	OOO	OOO	OOO	OOO
Saturday	OOO OOO	OOO	OOO	OOO	OOO	OOO
Sunday	OOO OOO	OOO	OOO	OOO	OOO	OOO

Figure 25.
Food diary
(Reproducible master in appendix)

Activity: Water Power

Why

To demonstrate the importance of water for living things

How

- Talk with students about the importance of water for the brain.

- Tell students they are going to do an experiment that will help them see the effects of water on living things.

■ Bring two plants (not cactus) into the classroom. Label one With Water and one Without Water. Have students observe the similarities between the two plants, noting the condition of the soil and the color and condition of the leaves. Water only one plant. Check daily to observe conditions of both plants. Ask students to draw conclusions and make connections between themselves and the plants.

Learning Link: How can I adapt this activity?

_____

_____

CHAPTER THIRTEEN

Cycles and Rhythms Activities

Take rest; a field that has rested gives a bountiful crop.

— Ovid

Activity: The State You're In

Why

To teach students about states and which states are optimal for learning

How

■ Talk with students about how everything they do is affected by the state they are in at that time. Ask them, "If you were asked to take out the garbage, when would you be more likely to do it—when you are flopped on the couch in front of the TV or when you're walking through the kitchen?" Explain that states of mind are made by the way you are thinking and the way you are feeling. Tell them that you are not going to ask them to take out the garbage, but you are going to ask them to do things that are dependent on a certain state.

■ List on the chalkboard or on a chart some positive learning states (confusion, challenge, curiosity, and self-convincer) and some negative learning states (frustration, apathy, and fear).

■ Talk with students about the meaning of the states and why some make learning easier and some make learning difficult.

Learning Link: How can I adapt this activity?

_____

_____

Activity: Name that State!

Note: We encourage students to recognize and manage their states.

Why

To help students recognize different states

How

- Talk with students about the importance of knowing what a positive learning state looks and feels like and what a negative learning state looks and feels like.

- Teach students to identify their own states:
    - relaxing
    - thinking/reflecting
    - active/moving
    - inhibiting

- Review the states with your students.

- Talk with students about how the states might look in regard to facial expressions, body language, and movement.

- Have students form groups of five or six members.

- Have one student leave the group while the rest of the students in the group decide which state they will act out. When the student returns, have him or her guess what state the group is acting out. (We played this at Eric Jensen's week-long course and loved it!)

- Make sure each student in the group gets a turn to "name that state!"

Learning Link: How can I adapt this activity?

_____

_____

Activity: State Changes

Why

To help students learn how to put themselves into a positive state for learning (this lesson works best if it is the third in the sequence on "states")

How

■ Review the learning states with students and talk about the importance of being in a state for learning. Tell the students that teachers try to get their students into a positive state by doing group activities. Even though teachers work on "state management" as best they can, ultimately, each student is responsible for the state he or she is in. Remind students that negative states can hinder their learning. Tell them that there are ways to change a negative state to a positive state—a state that will enhance their learning.

■ Brainstorm with the students activities that can be done in the classroom to put everyone into positive states. Some activities are:

   ■ listening to music

   ■ singing and dancing

   ■ doing a mind map

   ■ getting up and moving around

   ■ opening a window

   ■ playing games

   ■ Meaningful Mingling (see page 96)

   ■ closing eyes

   ■ GLP (see page 27)

   ■ Taking a Moment (see page 115)

   ■ exercising

   ■ getting a drink or eating a healthy snack

   ■ doing crossovers

   ■ going on a field trip

   ■ participating in a massage circle

   ■ having a guest speaker

   ■ reading

   ■ taking deep breaths

   ■ acting

   ■ laughing

   ■ playing

   ■ stretching

- doing group work

- going outside

- surprising others

■ Copy this list and post it where students can see it.

■ Ask the students which of the things on the list they can do on their own when they recognize their need to get into a positive state. Highlight or star those "state changes" students can do without disturbing others

Learning Link: How can I adapt this activity?

_____

_____

Activity: Staggered Show and Tell

Why

To build natural breaks into classroom routines so students get a burst of energy and a chance to be heard by an interested audience (It is not fair to presenters when their audience has become "numb" from sitting and listening for too long. It is not fair to expect the audience to stay focused for more than six speakers at a time.)

How

■ Ask students to present in groups of five or six, throughout the day or week.

■ Although this activity is called "show and tell," the strategy of breaking up presentation times can be used for presenting information, ideas, projects, or performances.

Learning Link: How can I adapt this activity?

_____

_____

Activity: Taking a Moment

Why

To give students a brain break

How

■ Talk with students about how busy school days can be and why it is important for them to have some time to collect their thoughts, reflect on what they have done, or have a moment when they do not have to think about anything. (Remind them that while they may feel like they are not thinking about anything, their brains are still working hard. Their brains may be processing something they dealt with hours or days ago.)

■ Be a "state manager"—watch your students closely and know when to "take a moment" with the whole group.

■ Invite students to "take a moment" when they need to. (Our students now say, "Excuse me, we need to 'take a moment.'") Encourage your students to be creative. Some students look like Rodin's *The Thinker*, or like John Cage in *Ally McBeal* when he pinches the bridge of his nose with his fingers.

Learning Link: How can I adapt this activity?

_____

_____

Activity: Song of the Week

Why

To signal action such as cleaning up, moving around, taking a quick break

How

■ Talk with students about the importance of having a signal— music, for example, can be one of the signals.

■ At the beginning of each week, gather students to listen to three or four selections of music. Have students choose, by voting with a show of hands, one song for the week. When the song is played throughout that week, it signals a specific action. If it is to signal a cleanup, the students know they need to be finished cleaning up by the time the song is over. If the signal is for a movement break, students often dance.

- When you are choosing the selections, make sure you use upbeat, lively tunes. Rock and roll is our students' (and Joy's) personal favorite. They also love the song "YMCA."

Learning Link: How can I adapt this activity?

_____

_____

Activity: Silent Birthday Line-Up

Why

To give a novel break that includes movement and thinking

How

- Talk with students about the value of breaks that include mental challenge as well as physical movement.

- Explain to students that they are to line up in order of their birthdays, starting with January, but they may not speak while they are forming the line.

- Give students time to form the line and then talk about how they managed to do it without talking.

Learning Link: How can I adapt this activity?

_____

_____

Activity: Playing Plates

Why

To give students an energizing break with music (Joy had the good fortune of doing this activity with Don Campbell, author of _The Mozart Effect_™. It was such fun, she does it with every group she works with.) In his book, Campbell talks about the value of listening to and moving with music. He claims that music by Mozart is particularly effective.

Note: In our experience, adults love this activity just as much as children.

How

- Talk with students about the power of music and the benefits of moving to music.

- Give students a pair of paper plates (the cheap ones work best).

- Tell students you are going to be the conductor and they need to follow what you do.

- Joy's favorite moves are: plates together in front of torso, plates banging together overhead, plates rubbing together off to the side, fanning face (and underarms)—you will soon create your own favorite moves.

- Put on the music and begin to conduct and play the plates.

- Give students a chance to conduct as well.

Learning Link: How can I adapt this activity?

_____

_____

Elimination of Threat Activities

Fear is the darkroom where negatives are developed.

— Anonymous

Activity: Cooperative News (Presentations)

Why

To give students a chance to communicate and be actively involved in a small group when there is a set amount of time

> *Learning is social—the more opportunities the better.*

How

- Talk with students about the value of working in cooperative groups.

- If your students are not already in cooperative groups, use your own system to put students into groups of four. (We set up the groups so that there is a balance of skills, interests, and personality styles.)

- Assign a role to each student in the group (for younger students, designate a recorder, an editor, a practice-coordinator/reporter, and an "Emily Post" position).

- Explain that the recorder will write on a large piece of chart paper what each person in the group shares or has to say; the editor/timer will keep time and will proofread, correct, and edit what has been written, then rewrite it on a 22 cm x 5 cm (8 1/2" x 2") strip of paper and glue it onto the master cooperative newsletter (see appendix); the practice-coordinator/reporter will have the students practice and will introduce their group; the student with the role of "Emily Post" makes sure students have a turn, listen

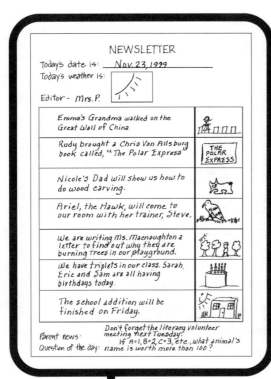

NEWSLETTER

Today's date is: _Nov. 23, 1999_

Today's weather is:

Editor - Mrs. P.

Emma's Grandma walked on the Great Wall of China.	
Rudy brought a Chris Van Allsburg book called, "The Polar Express"	THE POLAR EXPRESS
Nicole's Dad will show us how to do wood carving.	
Ariel, the Hawk, will come to our room with her trainer, Steve.	
We are writing Ms. Macnaughton a letter to find out why they are burning trees in our playground.	
We have triplets in our class. Sarah, Eric and Sam are all having birthdays today.	
The school addition will be finished on Friday.	

Parent news: Don't forget the literacy volunteer meeting next Tuesday.

Question of the day: If A=1, B=2, C=3, etc., what animal's name is worth more than 100?

Figure 26.
Cooperative
Newsletter
(Reproducible
master in appendix)

politely to each other without interruptions, use positive body language, and ask appropriate questions.

- Tell students they have ten minutes (depending on the task) to go to their "chosen" spot, sit facing each other, and complete sharing, recording, and reading their news.

- Ask students to come to the classroom meeting area and sit with their group in a large circle.

- Invite groups to stand and read their news together.

- The editor from each group proofreads, corrects, and edits (with peer or adult helpers) the news, and rewrites it on a strip of paper that is then glued onto the classroom "newsletter" (see figure 26).

- The newsletter is copied and sent home at the end of the day (we do cooperative news once or twice a week).

- With older students, the same strategy can be used to present research information and various opinions, or they can use it as a stage for rehearsal.

Learning Link: How can I adapt this activity?

_____

_____

Activity: Elevator

Why

To give students a strategy to help them deal with anger and stress

How

- Talk with students about what happens to us when we feel angry, frightened, worried, or stressed. Although our whole brain keeps working, we do not get as much blood to our frontal lobes, so we tend to react instead of think.

- Tell students you are going to teach them a strategy called Elevator, which they can use to calm themselves down and get control of their feelings.

- Model as you say to students: "Slowly and steadily take a deep breath through your nose and imagine you are going up in an elevator. You are at the first floor, second floor, third floor, fourth floor. At the fifth floor, hold your breath, close your eyes, and relax. Descend slowly and steadily, letting your breath out through your mouth till you are back at ground level." Repeat the process. As we talk students through this relaxation, our voices are calm and quiet.

- Talk with students about when they would use the Elevator strategy. Ask them to tell you about instances when it works for them.

Learning Link: How can I adapt this activity?

_____

_____

Activity: Test Smart

Why

To help students learn a variety of test-taking tactics

How

- Talk with students about test-taking anxiety and how even though they may know the content well, when they are working through a test, their minds may sometimes go blank. Tell the students there are some things they can do to help themselves. Some suggestions we have heard include:

  - Read over the whole test and plan your time.

  - Reread each question and say it in your own words.

  - Try different methods to trigger your memory—for example, web, pictures, lists.

  - Before the test, develop acronyms, pegging systems, and graphic organizers that you can use to help you recall.

  - Before you write a response, decide on your main ideas, then add supporting details.

  - Think of where you were when you learned the material.

- Look for patterns and see if that can help you tap into all of your intelligences. Ask, "Can I make a rap to help recall content?"

- Get enough sleep the night before a test. Make sure you have eaten, particularly protein, which helps thinking. Drink water.

- Take a few hard candies with you to give your blood sugar a boost.

■ Brainstorm with students what kinds of things they can do in class to help them remember. List them and have students make their own tips sheet for test-taking.

■ Have students organize their tips sheet in webs, lists, grids, and wallet cards.

■ Make a poster of the students' suggestions and post it on the classroom wall. Remind students to use their tips sheet when writing a test.

Learning Link: How can I adapt this activity?

Activity: Recognition

Why

To help students understand the value of authentic, varied, inclusive, and personal recognition

How

■ Talk with students about the ways people try to help others do their best by giving out prizes, treats, stickers, and other kinds of incentives and rewards. The brain does not work as well under threat. Worrying about receiving rewards can be threatening and interferes with learning—students will think about getting or not getting the reward instead of thinking about what they are working on. The brain needs feedback, however. It feels good to be recognized. Assure your young students they will get plenty of treats—it is important to celebrate!

■ Ask students what kinds of things they could do to recognize one another. The list we have seen includes: Specific Compliments (see page 66), 2 Hurrahs and a Hint (see page 64), writing each other positive notes, doing team cheers, giving "high fives" to one another, and singing an upbeat song or rap.

- Post the list and set aside time in class for students to recognize one another and share their recognition stories and feelings.

- Encourage your students to recognize their own efforts and accomplishments by giving them time to reflect, talk with others, and keep journals and learning logs.

Learning Link: How can I adapt this activity?

_____

_____

Activity: Rehearsal

Why

To help students be prepared and more confident

How

- Talk with students about how most people feel anxious about performing, presenting material, or even answering a question.

- Tell students there are things they can do to help them feel confident and ready to share. Each time they use the same pathways in their brain, the connections become stronger. One way to strengthen the connection is through practice. When they take time to rehearse, they not only get a chance to practice, they begin to feel more secure because they know they have done this before.

- Tell the students they can rehearse on their own, but when they practice with a partner or small group, they will get feedback that can help them fine-tune their work.

- As a teacher, you need to build practice and rehearsal time into your schedules to ensure your students are not put on the spot.

Learning Link: How can I adapt this activity?

_____

_____

Assessing Ourselves and Informing Others

For educators to be effective, we need to be reflective. We must each look at our practice and ask, "What am I doing that meets my vision of a brain-based classroom?"

We have found that our students' love of learning and their feelings of success are our best endorsements for brain-based learning. We have seen such positive results using the brain basics that we want our colleagues and the families of our students to gain an appreciation and enthusiasm for learning about the brain.

In this section, we include some materials we use that will help you add to your knowledge about brain-based learning. In chapter 15, we discuss how we assess brain-based learning in the classroom. In chapter 16, we offer some ways educators can assess their progress toward creating brain-compatible learning environments.

CHAPTER FIFTEEN

Assessing Brain-Based Learning

In our classrooms, we use the brain basics as an organizer for summarizing important information about the brain, for working with students, and for designing classroom activities. We also find the brain basics to be a useful assessment tool—for both student self-assessment and assessing our own practice. We have found the brain-basic bingo card (see appendix) to be the most effective self-assessment tool for our students. Recently, we heard Jane Hansen, author of *When Learners Evaluate*, talk about the necessity of having students identify their strengths so that they see themselves as readers and writers. When this is established, they can set realistic goals. For our own assessment, we use the brain-basic web (see appendix), a chart, or bingo card (see appendix), and ask ourselves:

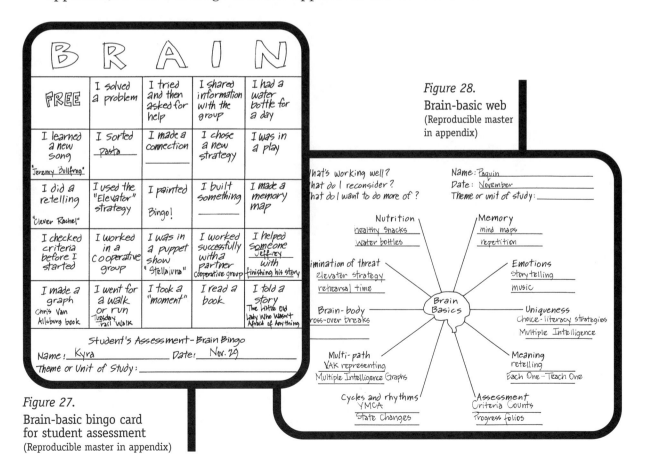

Figure 28.
Brain-basic web
(Reproducible master in appendix)

Figure 27.
Brain-basic bingo card
for student assessment
(Reproducible master in appendix)

B	R	A	I	N
Emotions "The Storm"	Threat "Snowball Fight"	Cycles and Rhythms "Playing Plates"	Multi-path VAK activity	Free Crazy Hat Day
Nutrition Water Bottles	Meaning storytelling (Clever Rachel)	Free Memory-Acronyms	Threat Rehearsal	Assessment "Criteria Counts"
Free FIELD TRIP! (to museum)	Brain-Body "Meaningful Mingling"	Memory Retelling activities	Free	Cycles and Rhythms "Name that State"
Unique M.I.T.	Memory meaning-memory maps	Emotions Compliment Chain	Nutrition video or presentation on veggies	Multi-path M.I. Graph
Brain-Body Cross-over breaks	Free	Unique Fan Letters	Assessment started "Snapshots on reading"	Meaning Each one-Teach one

BINGO - BRAIN BASICS

Name: _____ Date: _____

Theme or Unit of Study: _____

Figure 29.
Brain-basic
bingo card
(Reproducible master
in appendix)

■ What am I doing that is working well?

■ What do I want to reconsider or stop doing?

■ What do I want to do more of?

When we recently answered these questions, this is what we found: Colleen was pleased to note she was paying attention to all ten basics. She realized, however, that she wanted to monitor the amount of time she spent talking to students and, instead, add more breaks, movement, and music to her classroom's daily routines. Joy was pleased with how she had paid attention to the basics—except for nutrition. There had been too many parties with junk food, which everyone enjoyed just a little too much! From now on, every party will feature tofu snacks and plenty of veggies!

Another practical and effective way we have found to assess our teaching is to use the process for collecting authentic evidence as described in *British Columbia's Primary Program (Foundation Document)* (1991, 104). This process suggests that teachers observe their students, talk with them, and look at the products they create. Marilyn Chapman explains this process as, "Do, say, and make." We use this process as a mirror for our own practice and ask:

1. What activities do I see in the classroom that are brain compatible?

2. What language do I hear that supports a brain-friendly environment?

3. What products are the students making that show I am aware of and have respect for the unique ways they represent their knowledge?

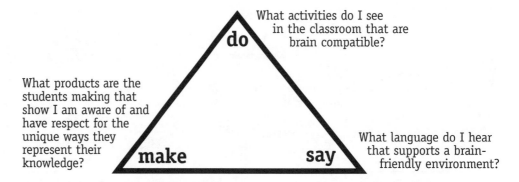

What activities do I see in the classroom that are brain compatible? — **do**

What language do I hear that supports a brain-friendly environment? — **say**

What products are the students making that show I am aware of and have respect for the unique ways they represent their knowledge? — **make**

We have provided a list of elements of a brain-compatible classroom that you can use to identify your strengths and see yourself as a brain-friendly educator. We find this process helpful when we match the points with a specific example from our classroom. Once you recognize your success, you can set goals for yourself and your classroom.

Uniqueness

- provide learner choice and variety
- provide opportunities to connect prior knowledge and experiences
- recognize learning styles, senses, and strengths

Assessment

- provide timely, specific feedback
- allow student and peer feedback
- allow personal reflection
- recognize mistakes as a positive part of learning

Emotions

- encourage appropriate use of emotions
- recognize that fun is part of learning
- recognize that play is crucial to learning
- use positive language

Meaning

- encourage holistic, integrated, thematic, relevant learning
- recognize personal relevance, patterns, and emotional content
- set aside large blocks of time for work
- provide time for processing and reflection

Multi-Path

- recognize multiple intelligences
- recognize multiple ways of presenting
- provide opportunities for varieties of representation
- enrich the environment with music, aromas, posters

Brain-Body

- encourage active learning
- take field trips, do demonstrations
- encourage movement

Memory

- use memory maps
- use peripherals
- provide many experiences

Nutrition

- encourage good food choices
- provide specific information about nutrition
- make water available at all times

Cycles and Rhythms

- make time for energizing activities
- recognize and manage students' states
- encourage the appropriate use of ritual, novelty, and challenge

Elimination of Threat

- manage stress
- provide a climate of respect
- make support available
- encourage intrinsic motivation; avoid awards

We invite you to identify and celebrate your successes. Add to this list as you discover additional ways to make your classroom more brain compatible. Once you have established your pattern of success, you can decide how you want to challenge yourself to create an even more brain-friendly classroom environment.

CHAPTER SIXTEEN

Informing Others

To help the families of our elementary-school students become more knowledgeable, we send them newsletters. The following is an example. Adapt it to fit your needs.

What's the Brain Got to Do With It? Information for Families

Dear Families:

Many of you have expressed interest in the work we have done in learning about the brain. You have asked for ideas so you can apply brain-based learning at home. Here is some information for you to consider. We have organized it by the ten points, or brain basics, we believe develop the most brain-friendly environment.

Uniqueness

Children's brains are as unique as their fingerprints. Each has his or her own genetic make-up and experiences that shape his or her brain. Just as children learn to walk, talk, and swim at different times, so do they learn to read, write, and use mathematical skills at different times. Children operate on their own internal time clocks, not on our time lines. For them to be successful, we need to give them time and their own experiences. Because each child is unique, it makes no sense to compare one to another. It does make sense to help each appreciate his or her own strengths. It is important to recognize the uniqueness of childhood; it is a stage when many parts of the brain, such as the frontal lobes—the center for reasoning and higher-level thinking—are still maturing.

Assessment

Children need to realize and appreciate what they are able to do—before they can improve. When we help children identify their accomplishments, we give them a base to build on and refine their skills. "Helpful hints" and criticism may actually hinder learning. When someone is threatened, his or her brain tends to go into a self-protective survival mode rather than keep energy focused in the frontal lobes where problem solving and creativity are centered. When we ask children to talk about their successes and give their own ideas for how they can improve, we lay the foundation for life-long achievement.

Emotions

Our emotions affect the quality of our thinking. When we are secure and happy, our brain releases positive neurotransmitters that allow it to make connections. When we are afraid or threatened, our brain releases inhibitory chemicals that make it more difficult for the cells to communicate. It is important to make sure children have a loving environment; it is a necessity for good learning. By teaching children to deal with their emotions, rather than be controlled by them, they become more successful learners.

Meaning

If something does not make sense, it is almost impossible to learn it. One of the main ways we make sense of new learning is to fit it into what we already know. This is why children constantly ask, "Why?" and it is why it is so important to learn skills in context. When we can see the big picture we can see how new learning is relevant and useful. When we take time to talk about a new topic before adding new information, we help learners activate a huge net of interconnected neurons that provide the foundation necessary for new learning to take place.

Multi-Path

Our brain receives information through all of our senses. We each have strengths in the ways we express our ideas. When we invite children to use all their senses by representing their thinking in a variety of ways, we give them more chances to "be smart." When we give children opportunities to dance, sing, act, learn to play a musical instrument, explore movement, participate in physical activities, and use art materials, we are helping them build skills that give them power to show what they know. The ability to express ideas in a variety of forms gives learners the rehearsal and confidence they need to use typical forms of communication such as writing.

Brain-Body

The quality of our thinking depends on the quality of the food we eat, how much water we drink, how much sleep we get, and how much we exercise. When children eat a balanced diet, they have the raw materials they need to produce the brain chemicals necessary for learning. Water is necessary to maintain the chemical balance in the brain, so we encourage children to drink water throughout the day. Sleep is critical so our brain can "sort" and "catalog" our memories. Exercise supplies our brain with oxygenated blood, giving us a sense of well being, relaxation, and efficiency. One workshop leader we had says, "Move them and they will learn."

Memory

If we want children to remember what we want them to learn, we have to do more than simply tell them—telling involves only one memory system. When we plan activities, we involve other memory systems. The more ways we learn something, the better chance we have of being able to recall it later. Most people recall from five to seven items at a time, plus or minus two. For young children, this number is lower so instead of giving them a "laundry list" of things to do, we give directions in manageable chunks of one or two. This avoids frustration for both them and ourselves. We know that emotion has the effect of setting memories in our brain so we try to build a learning community that is safe, positive, and enjoyable.

Nutrition

All parents want their children to eat a balanced diet. At school, we try to support this goal by teaching our students about foods that help their brains function in top form. Eating protein at breakfast, for example, helps us think clearly and remain alert. Foods like bread and pasta are necessary for our brain to produce serotonin, a substance that helps us to be calm. Fruits and vegetables supply the vitamins and minerals our brain needs for nerve development and healthy brain function. Dairy products are a source of calcium and produce calpain, a cleaner for the synapses in our brain. We encourage our students to drink water. Our brain is comprised of over 70 percent water—when we are dehydrated, our thinking is affected. We tell our students that they should drink soda pop and sugar-based drinks only on occasion—these drinks rob the body of water and contain chemicals that can make us perform poorly.

Cycles and Rhythms

Our brain runs on cycles of attention based on our natural rhythms and sleep cycles. In a classroom with twentysome students, we realize everyone must be at a different point in their attention cycle so we do activities such as games and breaks that put children in a positive state for learning. (At home, we have learned it does not pay to ask a son or daughter to do a job when he or she is flopped out in front of the TV. The best time to take out the garbage, for example, is when a child is already up and moving. Then "please take out the garbage" is a reasonable request that doesn't lead to a battle.) Children also need downtime— plain old undirected play—when they can relax and their brains have time to process what they have learned. Sports and lessons are wonderful for children, but it is important to be selective about the number of activities children are involved in. School, plus several other activities, can leave children with such busy schedules that they are always in the high point of a cycle and not getting the processing time they need to make their learning last.

Elimination of Threat

When we feel threatened, our brain does not work as well; we are using our thinking power for basic survival rather than for problem solving. When we are stressed, angry, or upset, our large muscles tense and our eyes scan for danger—it is hard to focus on a small area like a page of print. Children need to know that they are loved unconditionally and have allies who will advocate for them and help deal with dilemmas. One hidden source of threat we try to remove from our classrooms is awards, rewards, prizes, bribes, and comparisons. When we try to motivate children with words such as "If you do this, you'll get that," it may work in the short run. We know, however, that the survival-oriented brain tends to focus on the prize rather than on the learning. Our brain likes to feel in control and responds positively to choice by producing chemicals that actually help to set memory. Rewards take away that sense of choice, so we help children recognize and celebrate their efforts and accomplishments in ways that do not interfere with learning.

We hope you find these ideas interesting and useful for promoting learning in your home. It is wonderful to hear children talking about how their brains work and how they can help themselves use this information to be better learners. We are confident you will also enjoy hearing "brain bytes" from your children.

Sincerely,

When we work with older students, we use the same format and adapt the letter to make it more age appropriate. We also challenge our students to use this format, or design their own format, to provide their families with information about brain-based learning in their classroom.

With our colleagues, we try to share information by loaning books and materials from our "brain collection," trading classes to teach a unit on the brain, and conducting workshops for teachers. Colleen has formed a group of interested educators who meet monthly to share books, materials, and ideas. Some people belong to book clubs; she belongs to a "brain club."

We find the best ambassadors for brain-based learning are our students. They delight in dazzling their next-year teachers with "brain facts." Sometimes their teachers come to us and request ideas for continuing the brain research. We are delighted to oblige.

Conclusion

*A real voyage of discovery comes not from seeking
new landscapes, but from having new eyes.*

— Proust

Some Final Words and Wishes

We began this book by looking at WIIFM. We ended it with some new discoveries. Colleen has theory to support her practice and Joy understands why some activities are so successful. Each of us has found that approaching our teaching from the brain-based perspective has given us new energy, enthusiasm, and challenge. Some people have said, "This brain-based learning is just common sense and it's what good teachers do anyway!" We agree. The power for us has come from understanding and appreciating learning from a new perspective and from using the brain basics as the principles that serve as a foundation for enhancing teaching and learning.

Like all learners, educators are unique individuals. Some of us "jump in with both feet" and some of us need to take "baby steps." Each of us needs to do what is right for ourself in our situation. Just as we have respect for our students, we need to respect and appreciate our own individuality as learners.

We hope this book has given you useful information and practical activities you can adapt for your students. Our wish is that you share our excitement in learning more about the brain and apply that information to your life and learning.

Bibliography

Armstrong, Thomas. *Awakening Your Child's Natural Genius: Enhancing Curiosity, Creativity, and Learning Ability*. Los Angeles, CA: J. P. Tarcher, 1991.

Anthony, Robert J. et al. *Evaluating Literacy*. Concord, ON: Irwin Publishing, 1991.

Barlow, Bob. *Bob Barlow's Book of Brain Boosters*. New York: Scholastic, 1997.

Bellanca, James. *Active Learning Handbook: For the Multiple Intelligence's Classroom*. Arlington Heights, IL: Skylight, 1997.

Brownlie, Faye, and Catherine Feniak. *Student Diversity*. Markham, ON: Pembroke Publishers, 1998.

Bruner, J. *The Culture of Education*. Cambridge, MA: Harvard University Press, 1996.

Caine, Renate, and Geoffrey Caine. *Education on the Edge of Possibility*. Alexandria, VA: ASCD, 1997a.

———. *Unleashing the Power of Perceptual Change*. Alexandria, VA: ASCD, 1997b.

———. *Making Connections: Teaching and the Human Brain*. Alexandria, VA: ASCD, 1991.

Caine, Geoffrey, Renate Caine, and Sam Crowell. *MindShifts*. Tucson, AZ: Zephyr Press, 1994.

Cameron, Caren et al. *Recognition Without Rewards*. Winnipeg, MB: Peguis Publishers, 1997.

Calvin, William H. *How Brains Think: Evolving Intelligence, Then and Now*. New York: Basic Books, 1996.

Chapman, Marilyn. *Weaving Webs of Meaning*. Toronto, ON: Nelson, 1997.

Costa, Arthur, James Bellanca, and Robin Fogarty, eds. *If Minds Matter: A Foreword to the Future*. Palatine, IL: Skylight,1992.

Damasio, Antonio R. *Descartes' Error: Emotion, Reason, and the Human Brain*. New York: Avon Books, 1994.

Davies, Anne et al. *Together Is Better: Collaborative Assessment, Evaluation & Reporting.* Winnipeg, MB: Peguis Publishers, 1992.

Dennison, Paul E., and Gail E. Dennison. *Brain Gym Teachers Edition.* Ventura, CA: Edu-Kinesthetics, 1989.

DePorter, Bobbi, and Mike Hernacki. *Quantum Learning: Unleashing the Genius in You.* New York: Dell, 1992.

Diamond, Marian, and Janet Hopson. *Magic Trees of the Mind: How to Nuture Your Child's Intelligence, Creativity, and Health Emotions from Birth Through Adolescence.* New York: Dutton, 1998.

Donovan, Priscilla, and Jacquelyn Wonder. *The Forever Mind: Eight Ways to Unleash the Powers of Your Mature Mind.* New York: W. Morrow, 1994.

Dryden, Gordon. *Out of the Red.* Auckland, NZ: Collins, 1978.

Fogarty, Robin. *Brain-Compatible Classrooms.* Arlington Heights, IL: Skylight Training and Publishing, 1997.

Frischknecht, Jacqueline, and Glenn Capelli. *Maximizing Your Learning Potential.* Winnipeg, MB: Skills of Learning, 1995.

Gardner, Howard. *Creating Minds: An Anatomy of Creativity Seen Through the Lives of Freud, Einstein, Picasso, Stravinsky, Eliot, Graham, and Gandhi.* New York: Basic Books, 1993.

———. *Multiple Intelligences.* New York: Basic Books, 1993.

Goleman, Daniel. *Emotional Intelligence.* New York: Bantam Books, 1995.

Greenfield, Susan A. *The Human Brain: A Guided Tour.* New York: Basic Books, 1997.

Gregory, Kathleen, Caren Cameron, and Anne Davies. *Setting and Using Criteria: For Use in Middle and Secondary School Classrooms.* Merville, BC: Connections Publishing, 1997.

Hannaford, Carla. *Smart Moves: Why Learning Is Not All In Your Head.* Arlington, VA: Great Ocean Publishers, 1995.

Hart, Leslie A. *Human Brain and Human Learning.* New York: Longman, 1983.

Hoffman, Donald D. *Visual Intelligence: How We Create What We See.* New York: W.W. Norton, 1998.

Howard, Pierce J. *The Owner's Manual for the Brain: Everyday Applications from Mind-Brain Research.* Austin, TX: Bard Press, 1999.

Ingram, Jay. *The Burning House: Unlocking the Mysteries of the Brain.* Toronto, ON: Penguin Books, 1995.

Jensen, Eric. *Introduction to Brain-Compatible Learning.* San Diego, CA: The Brain Store, 1998a.

———. *Teaching With the Brian in Mind.* Alexandria, VA: ASCD, 1998b.

———. *Brain-Compatible Strategies.* San Diego, CA: The Brain Store, 1997.

———. *Completing the Puzzle: The Brain-Based Approach.* San Diego, CA: The Brain Store, 1996.

———. *Brain-Based Learning & Teaching.* San Diego, CA: The Brain Store, 1995a.

———. *Super Teaching.* San Diego, CA: The Brain Store, 1995b.

———. *The Learning Brain.* San Diego, CA.: The Brain Store, 1995c.

Kirby, Dan, and Carol Kuykendall. *Mind Matters: Teaching for Thinking.* Portsmouth, NH: Boynton/Cook, 1991.

Kline, Peter, and Laurence D. Martel. *School Success: The Inside Story.* Arlington, VA: Great Ocean Publishers, 1992.

Kohn, Alfie. *The Schools Our Children Deserve.* New York: Houghton Mifflin, 1999.

———. *What to Look For in a Classroom.* San Francisco: Jossey Bass, 1998.

Kotulak, Ronald. *Inside the Brain: Revolutionary Discoveries of How the Mind Works.* Kansas City, MO: Andrews and McMeel, 1996.

Kovalik, Susan. *ITI, The Model: Integrated Thematic Instruction.* Kent, WA: Susan Kovalik & Associates, 1994.

Langer, Ellen J. *The Power of Mindful Learning.* Reading, MA: Addison-Wesley, 1997.

LeDoux, Joseph. *The Emotional Brain: The Mysterious Underpinnings of Emotional Life.* New York: Simon & Schuster, 1996.

Lincoln, Wanda, and Murray Suid, comp. *The Teacher's Quotation Book.* Palo Alto, CA: Dale Seymour Publications, 1986.

Ministry of Education, Province of British Columbia. *Primary Program (Foundation Document (6C0279)).* Victoria, 1991.

Ornstein, Robert. *The Evolution of Consciousness: Of Darwin, Freud, and Cranial Fire: The Origins of the Way We Think.* New York: Prentice Hall Press, 1991.

Pert, Candace. *Molecules of Emotion: Why You Feel the Way You Feel.* New York: Scribner, 1997.

Politano, Colleen, and Anne Davies. *Multi-Age and More.* Winnipeg, MB: Peguis Publishers, 1994.

Promislow, Sharon. *Making the Brain/Body Connection.* North Vancouver, BC: Kinetic Publishing, 1997.

Ramachandran, V.S., and Susan Blakeslee. *Phantoms in the Brain: Probing the Mysteries of the Human Mind.* New York: W. Morrow, 1998.

Restak, Richard, M. *The Mind.* New York: Bantam, 1998.

———. *Brainscapes.* New York: Hyperion, 1995.

———. *The Modular Brain.* New York: Touchtone, 1995.

———. *Receptors.* New York: Bantam, 1994.

———. *The Brain Has a Mind of Its Own.* New York: Crown Publishers, 1991.

———. *The Brain: The Last Frontier.* New York: Doubleday, 1979.

Robertson, Dr. Joel C., and Tom Monte. *Peak-Performance Living.* San Francisco: Harper, 1996.

Russell, Peter. *The Brain Book.* New York: Penguin, 1979.

Schacter, Daniel L. *Searching for Memory.* New York: Basic Books, 1996.

Sprenger, Marilee. "Memory Lane Is a Two-Way Street." *Educational Leadership* (November 1998).

———. *Learning & Memory: The Brain in Action.* Alexandria, VA: ASCD, 1999.

Sternberg, Robert J. *Successful Intelligence.* New York: Simon & Schuster, 1996.

Sylwester, Robert. "Art for the Brain's Sake." *Educational Leadership* (November 1998).

———. *A Celebration of Neurons.* Alexandria, VA: ASCD, 1995.

Sylwester, Robert. ed. *Student Brains, School Issues: A Collection of Articles.* Arlington Heights, IL: Skylight, 1998.

Wade, Nicholas, ed. *The Science Times Book of the Brain.* New York: Lyons Press, 1998.

Children's Books

Biesty, Stephen. *Stephen Biesty's Incredible Body Book*. Markham, ON: Dorling Kindersley, 1998.

Dryden, Gordon, and Jeannette Vos. *The Learning Revolution*. Winnipeg, MB: Skills of Learning, 1994.

Feuring, Barb. *Braindance Presenter's Guide*. Surrey, BC: Cutting Education Publishers, 1998.

Funston, Sylvia, and Jay Ingram. *The Kid's Guide to the Brain*. Toronto, ON: Greey de Pencier Books, 1994.

Parker, Steve. *Brain Surgery for Beginners*. Brookfield, CT: The Millbrook Press, 1993.

———. *Human Body*. London: Dorling Kindersley, 1993.

Simon, Seymour. *The Brain*. New York: Scholastic, 1997.

Treays, Rebecca et. al. *Understanding Your Brain*. Tulsa, OK: Usborne, 1996.

Western, Joan, and Ronald Wilson. *The Human Body*. Mahwah, NJ: Troll Associates, 1991.

Williams, Frances. *Human Body*. Willowdale, ON: Firefly Books, 1997.

A P P E N D I X
Black Line Masters

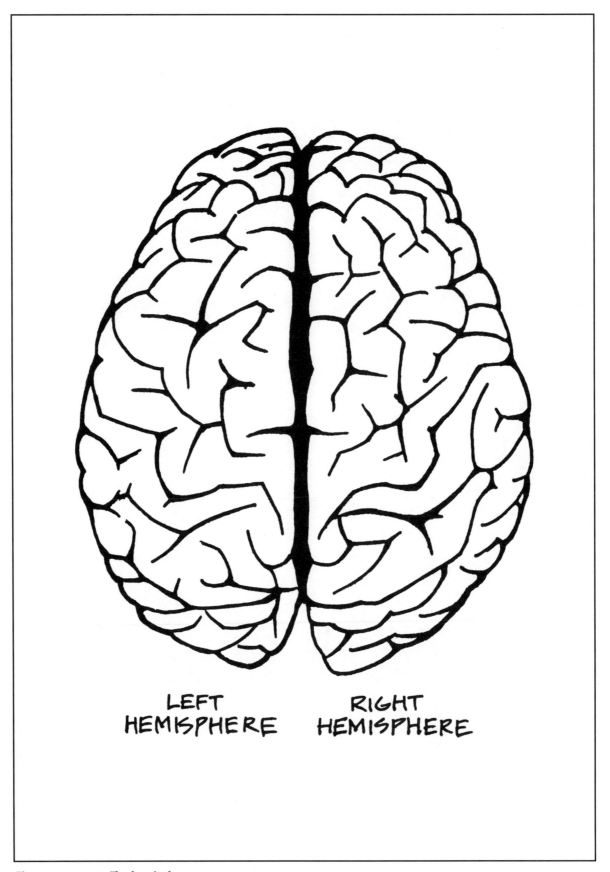

LEFT
HEMISPHERE

RIGHT
HEMISPHERE

Figure 1, page 7: The hemispheres

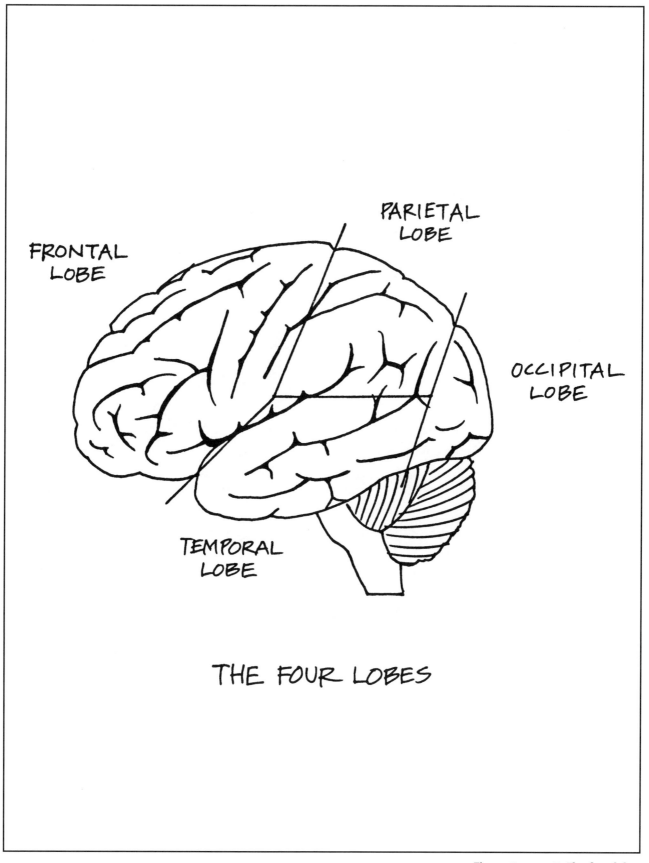

FRONTAL
LOBE

PARIETAL
LOBE

OCCIPITAL
LOBE

TEMPORAL
LOBE

THE FOUR LOBES

Figure 2, page 7: The four lobes

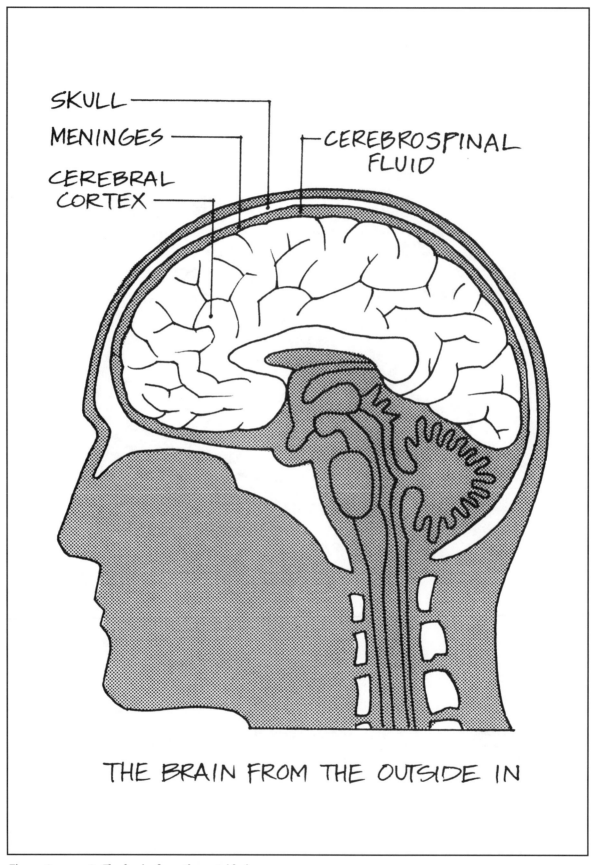

SKULL

MENINGES

CEREBRAL
CORTEX

CEREBROSPINAL
FLUID

THE BRAIN FROM THE OUTSIDE IN

Figure 3, page 8: The brain from the outside in

Brain-Based Learning With Class

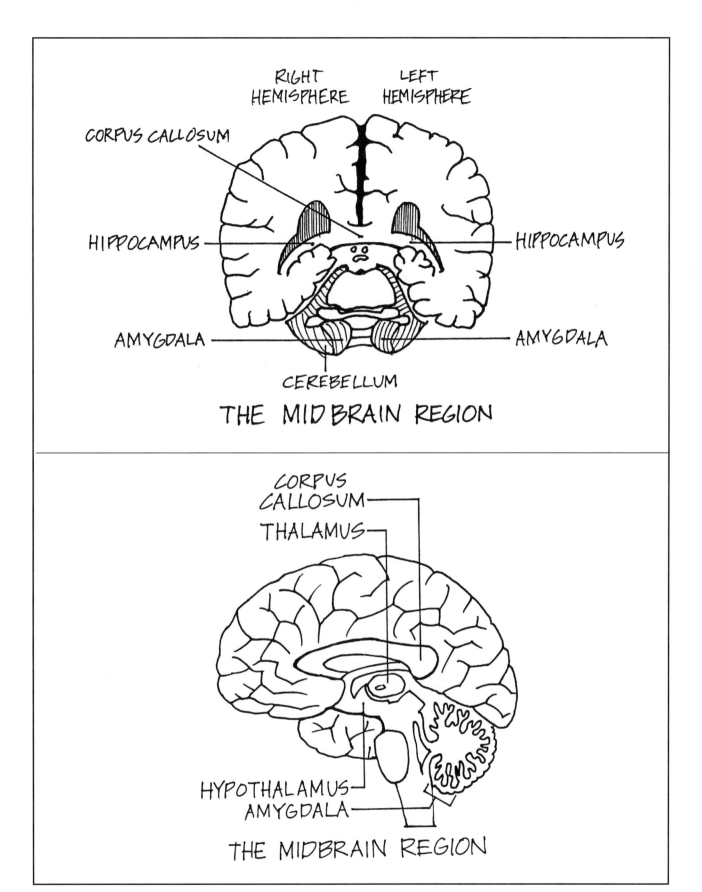

Figure 4, page 8: The midbrain region

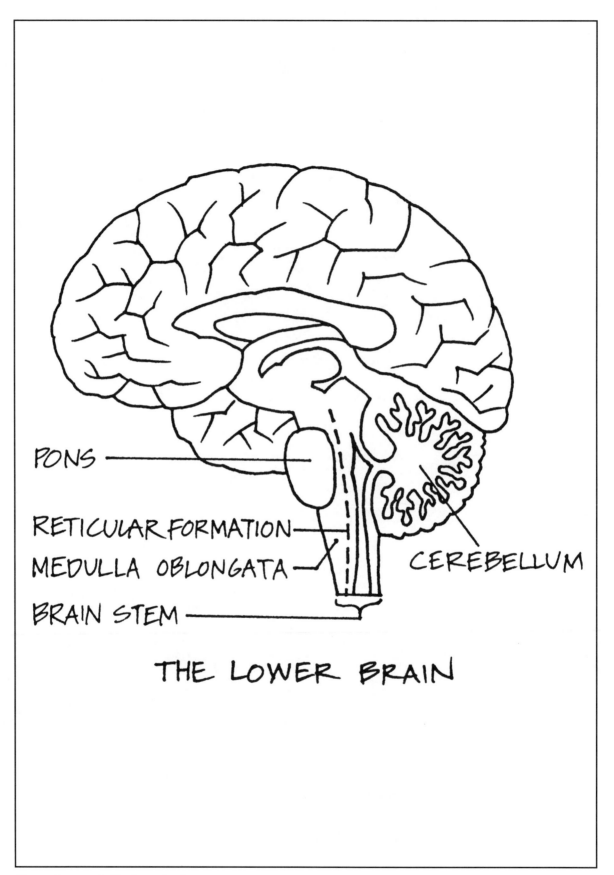

PONS

RETICULAR FORMATION

MEDULLA OBLONGATA

BRAIN STEM

CEREBELLUM

THE LOWER BRAIN

Figure 5, page 9: The lower brain

Brain-Based Learning With Class

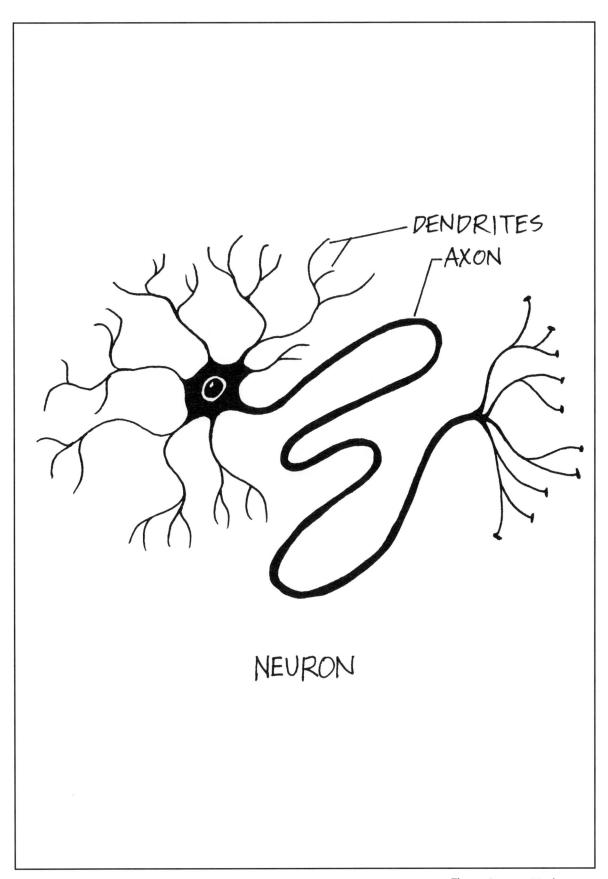

DENDRITES

AXON

NEURON

Figure 6, page 11: A neuron

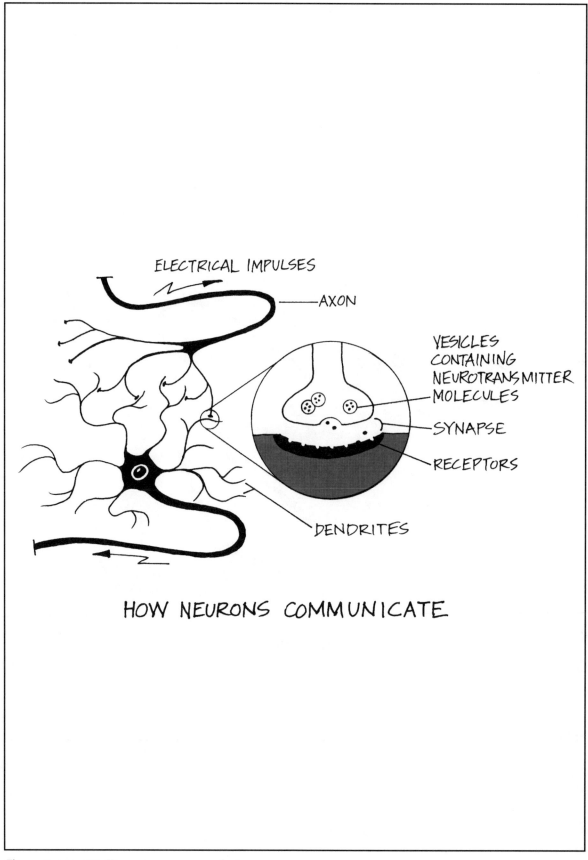

Figure 7, page 12: How neurons communicate

Date _____   Name _____

How is your brain like...?

a cabbage

a raisin

a pillowcase

a grapefruit

an avocado/porridge

string cheese

a walnut

Figure 9, page 40: How is your brain like...?

The Pegging System

#1: sun: There is only one sun.

#2: eyes, ears: We have two eyes and two ears.

#3: three pigs: In the story *The Three Little Pigs*, the pigs were happy, sad, and fearful.

#4: table: A table has four legs.

#5: five senses: We have five senses.

#6: sticks: Five, six, pick up sticks.

#7: telephone: There are seven digits in a telephone number.

#8: snowman: A snowman is shaped like the number eight.

#9: baseball: There are nine players on the field and nine innings in the game.

#10: countdown: Countdown for a blastoff!

Figure 10, page 48: The pegging system

Brain-Based Learning With Class

B	R	A	I	N
GUEST LECTURE	LITERATURE CONNECTION:	IMAGERY	LECTURE	ROLE PLAYING
MEANING AND MEMORY MAPS	VIDEOS	MUSIC	INTERVIEWING	MATH CONNECTION
DEMONSTRATION	DEBATE	FIELD TRIPS	TECHNOLOGY	STUDENT PRESENTATIONS
CENTERS:	STORYTELLING	EXPERIMENT	DRAMA	POETRY
ARTIFACTS	JIGSAW AN ARTICLE	PROBLEM SOLVING	WIIFM/ SWYAK	GAMES

PRESENTATION BRAIN BINGO

DATE _____ THEME OR UNIT OF STUDY _____

Figure 12, page 61: Presentation brain bingo sheet

To _____

Hurrah!

Hurrah!

Hint...

From _____

To _____

Hurrah!

Hurrah!

Hint...

From _____

To _____

Hurrah!

Hurrah!

Hint...

From _____

To _____

Hurrah!

Hurrah!

Hint...

From _____

Figure 13, page 64: 2 hurrahs and a hint

Brain-Based Learning With Class

To _____   **From** _____

Two Stars

⭐

⭐

A Wish

Figure 14, page 64: 2 stars and a wish

_____'s Appointment Book

8:00 _____

9:00 _____

10:00 _____

11:00 _____

12:00 _____

1:00 _____

2:00 _____

Figure 16, page 76: Appointment book A

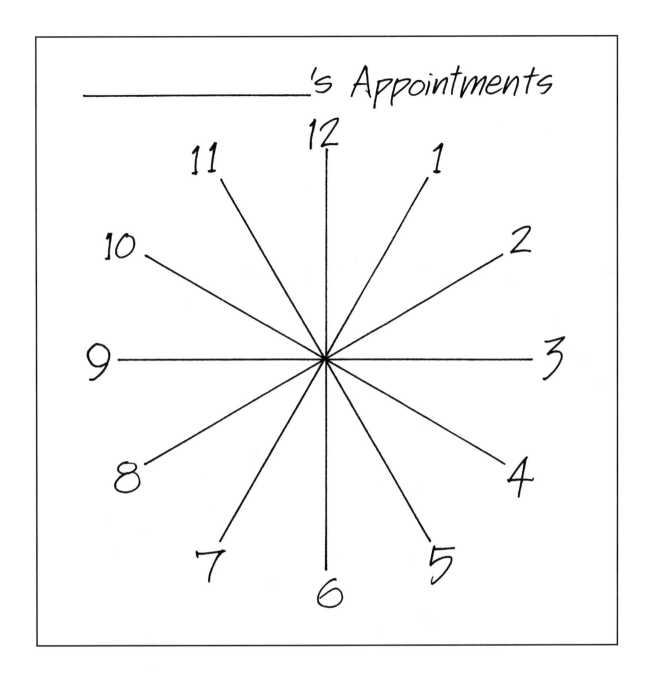

_____'s Appointments

Figure 17, page 76: Appointment book B

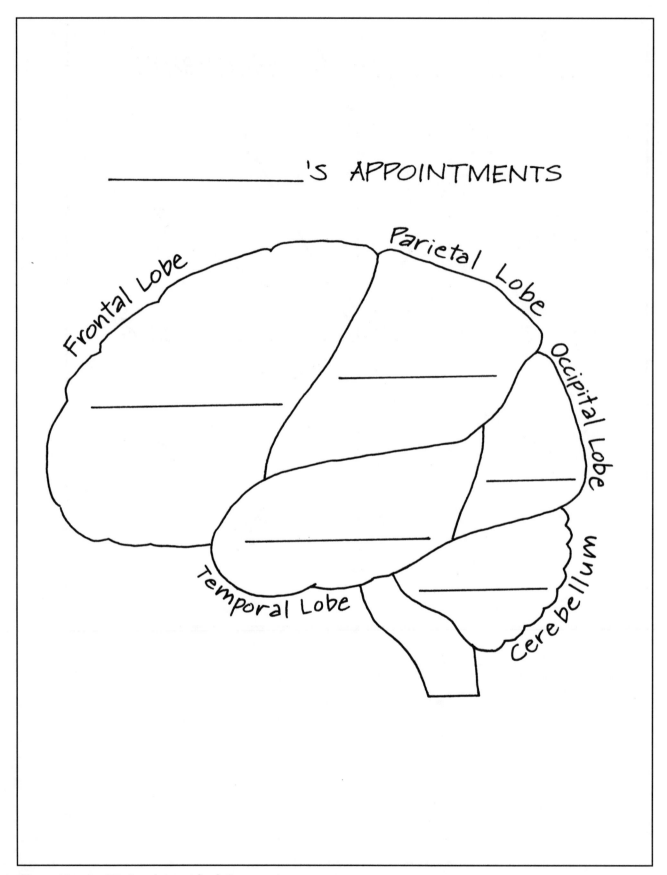

_____'S APPOINTMENTS

Frontal Lobe

Parietal Lobe

Occipital Lobe

Temporal Lobe

Cerebellum

Figure 18, page 77: Appointment book C

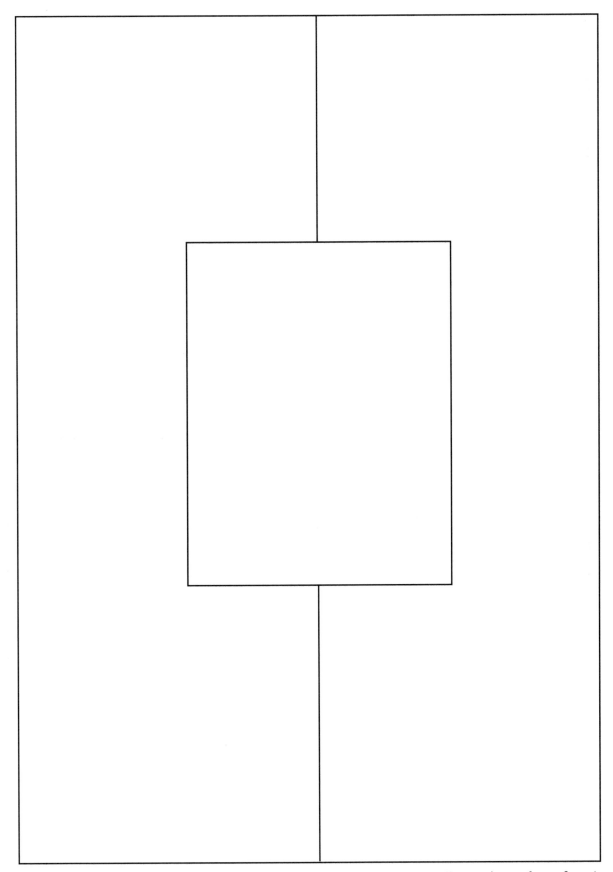

Figure 19, page 79: Yours, mine, and ours form A

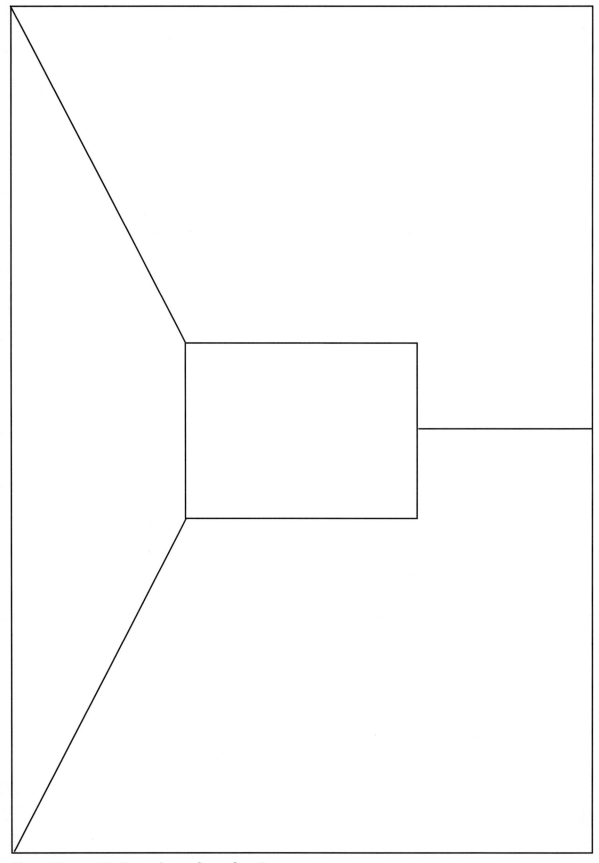

Figure 20, page 79: Your, mine, and ours form B

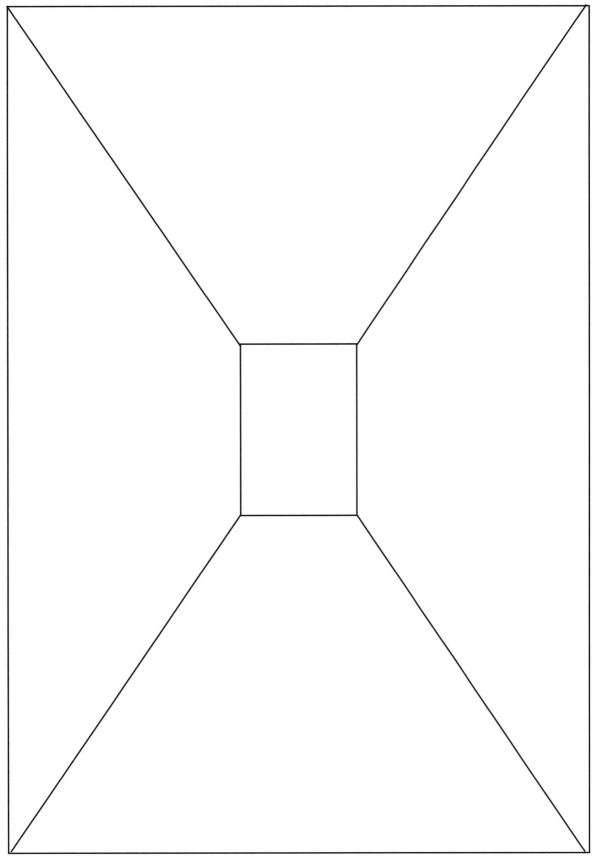

Figure 21, page 79: Yours, mine, and ours form C

Learning Senses

Visual Learner

- learns best from visual information
- observes details around him or her
- usually does not find noise distracting
- finds it easier to remember what he or she sees
- likes to make eye contact

- speaks quickly
- makes mental pictures
- tends to remember what he or she sees rather than what he or she hears
- is often a good speller
- prefers to read rather than be read to
- enjoys writing
- likes to look at artwork

- tends to doodle
- prefers to give a demonstration rather than give a speech
- may forget to pass on a verbal message
- needs the big purpose and a sense of purpose
- needs instructions and materials to be written as well as given verbally

Auditory Learner

- learns best from verbal information
- talks to himself/herself
- usually finds noise distracting
- finds it easier to remember what he or she hears
- tends to be talkative; relishes discussions

- speaks rhythmically with tone, pitch, and volume
- is able to mimic speech patterns and sounds
- tends to be an eloquent speaker
- often reviews conversations mentally
- is more able to spell orally than in writing

- likes to read aloud and listen
- enjoys listening to music
- prefers to express his or her ideas orally
- likes jokes better than comics
- prefers to tell information rather than write it down

Kinesthetic Learner

- learns best from physical input
- likes to move and be active
- finds it easier to remember what he or she does physically
- often touches others to get their attention
- speaks slowly

- memorizes by walking and doing
- large muscles develop early
- tracks print with finger when he or she is reading
- does better by doing a task rather than by reading or hearing about it
- handwriting may be messy

- likes games and drama
- uses action words
- uses gestures to communicate
- finds it difficult to sit still
- needs action
- prefers to use the body to show what he or she knows
- likes to be comfortable

Figure 22, page 84: Characteristics of visual, auditory, and kinesthetic learners

Brain-Based Learning With Class

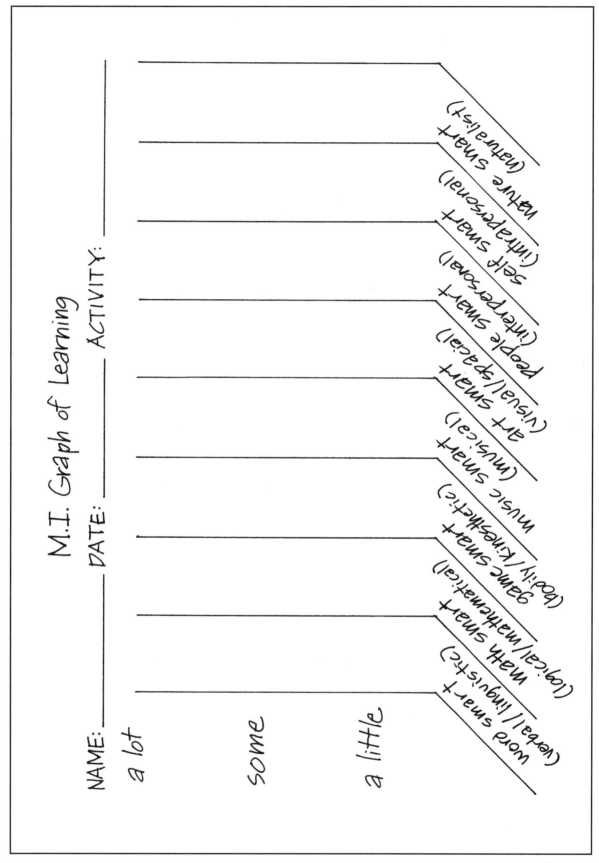

M.I. Graph of Learning

NAME: _____

DATE: _____ ACTIVITY: _____

	a lot	some	a little
word smart (verbal/linguistic)			
math smart (logical/mathematical)			
game smart (bodily/kinesthetic)			
music smart (musical)			
art smart (visual/spatial)			
people smart (interpersonal)			
self smart (intrapersonal)			
nature smart (naturalist)			

Figure 23, page 90: M.I. graph of learning

Food Diary

When you eat or drink - write it in your diary.
Fill in the circles so you can see that you are getting a balanced diet.

	Water	Protein	Milk products	Fruits	Vegetables	Grains
Monday	OOO OOO OOO	OOO	OOO	OOO	OOO	OOO
Tuesday	OOO OOO OOO	OOO	OOO	OOO	OOO	OOO
Wednesday	OOO OOO OOO	OOO	OOO	OOO	OOO	OOO
Thursday	OOO OOO OOO	OOO	OOO	OOO	OOO	OOO
Friday	OOO OOO OOO	OOO	OOO	OOO	OOO	OOO
Saturday	OOO OOO OOO	OOO	OOO	OOO	OOO	OOO
Sunday	OOO OOO OOO	OOO	OOO	OOO	OOO	OOO

Figure 25, page 109: Food diary

Brain-Based Learning With Class

NEWSLETTER

Today's date is: _____

Today's weather is:

Editor –

Parent news:

Question of the day:

Figure 26, page 120: Cooperative newsletter

B R A I N

FREE	I solved a problem	I tried and then asked for help	I shared information with the group	I had a water bottle for a day
I learned a new song _____	I sorted _____	I made a connection _____	I chose a new strategy	I was in a play
I did a retelling	I used the "Elevator" strategy	I painted	I built something _____	I made a memory map
I checked criteria before I started	I worked in a cooperative group	I was in a puppet show	I worked successfully with a partner	I helped someone _____ with _____
I made a graph	I went for a walk or run	I took a "moment"	I read a book	I told a story

Student's Assessment – Brain Bingo

Name: _____ Date: _____

Theme or Unit of Study: _____

Figure 27, page 127: Brain-basic bingo card for student assessment

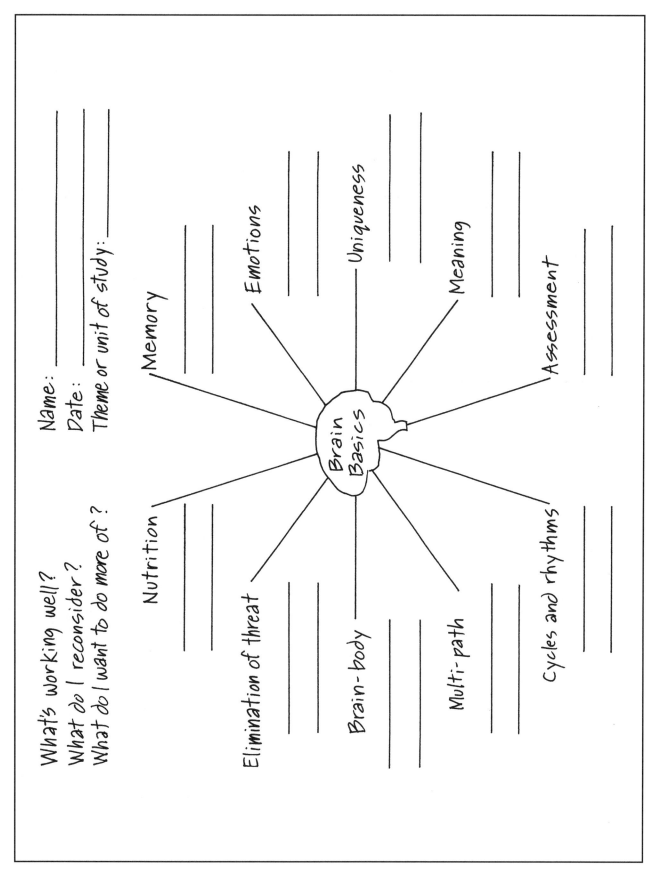

What's working well?
What do I reconsider?
What do I want to do more of?

Name: _____
Date: _____
Theme or unit of study: _____

Memory

Emotions

Uniqueness

Meaning

Assessment

Cycles and rhythms

Multi-path

Brain-body

Elimination of threat

Nutrition

Brain Basics

Figure 28, page 127: Brain-basic web

B	R	A	I	N
Emotions	Threat	Cycles and Rhythms	Multi-path	Free
Nutrition	Meaning	Free	Threat	Assessment
Free	Brain-Body	Memory	Free	Cycles and Rhythms
Unique	Memory	Emotions	Nutrition	Multi-path
Brain-Body	Free	Unique	Assessment	Meaning

BINGO - BRAIN BASICS

Name: _____ Date: _____

Theme or Unit of Study: _____

Figure 29, page 128: Brain-basic bingo card

Colleen Politano and Joy Paquin are available to do workshops and institutes on brain-based learning. If you enjoyed this book, you'll love their workshops.

Here's what participants are saying:

" A worthwhile day! I'm certainly encouraged to do more work and study on brain-based learning."

" Your energy was contagious! Wow!"

" Terrific presentation. Great strategies to take home and use in school."

" Enthusiastic. Energetic. Interesting. Entertaining. So knowledgeable about the topic."

" Excellent presentation, variety, pacing. You've excited me to pursue this area."

For more information, please contact Portage & Main Press (Peguis Publishers) at
1-800-667-9673.

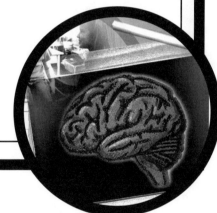

If you are as captivated with learning about the brain as we are, you will be searching for new materials. Our favorite source is The Brain Store. Their catalog contains the most current information and products available. You can contact The Brain Store in the following ways:

- **By mail:**

  The Brain Store
  4202 Sorrento Valley Blvd., Ste. B,
  San Diego, CA
  USA 92121

- **By phone:**

  1-800-325-4769 (US only)
  1-858-546-7555

- **By fax:**

  1-858-546-7560

- **Or visit The Brain Store web site:**

  http://www.thebrainstore.com

The
Brain
Store